Wyatt Earp
The little ship with many names

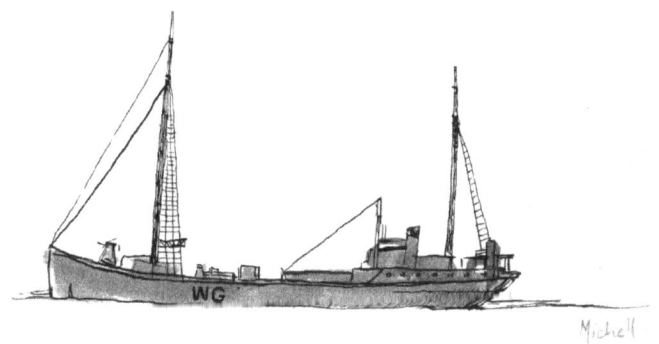

TRISH BURGESS

Wyatt Earp: The little ship with many names. | Trish Burgess

ISBN: 9781925826937

Published in 2020 by Connor Court Publishing Pty Ltd.

Copyright © Trish Burgess.

Not to be reproduced without the permission of the copyright holders.

Connor Court Publishing Pty Ltd
PO Box 7257
Redland Bay QLD 4165

sales@connorcourt.com
www.connorcourtpublishing.com.au

Printed in Australia

Cover and page layout by Graham Lindsay.

Cover art and other sketches were created by © Matilda Michell.

Back cover photo of the author © Andrew Blyth.

All photos have credits in the captions.

Wyatt Earp

The little ship with many names

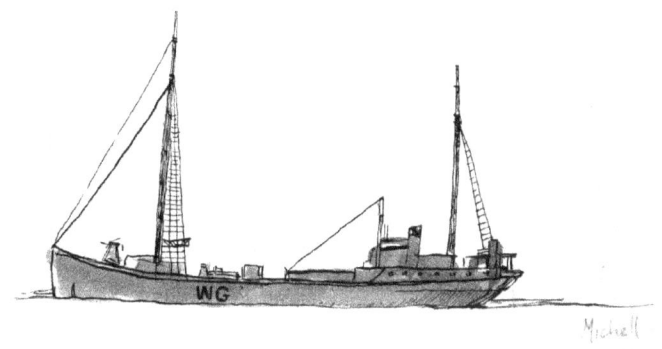

TRISH BURGESS

Connor Court Publishing   2020

Acknowledgements

First and foremost my thanks to everyone who has contributed in any way to this book. I have had nothing but friendly, cooperative and useful responses to all my requests—large and small—for information and help, and great encouragement from many friends!

At the top of a long list must be my friend and colleague at UNSW Canberra's Howard Library, Professor Tom Frame AM. Thanks to Tom, for his enthusiasm for this book, his support, his comments and his suggestions. And the occasional Tim Tam! Thanks too to my friends, the other supportive members of the Howard Library, Annette Carter and Andrew Blyth, who also like a chocolate or three.

Kenneth Staurset Fåne, the Curator at the Romsdal Museum in Molde, Norway, was incredibly helpful, providing access to many photographs and finding and/or confirming information about the early life of *Fanefjord*, and patiently answering many questions! My thanks are further extended to the Romsdal Museum for allowing me to use some of their photographs as well as some from Magnus Johannessen's photo albums which they hold.

Thanks to Professor John Nethercote for his editing expertise and to friends for many years, Dr Bruce Moore and Dr Ian Norman, who gave their time and experience in reading and commenting on drafts as well as being keen and supportive. And more thanks to Graham Lindsay for his incredible typesetting knowledge and skills.

Mr John Perryman, Director, Strategic and Historical Studies of the Naval History Section at Sea Power Centre—Australia, Department of Defence, was extremely helpful in allowing me access to the *Wyatt Earp* files and photographs held by his Section and, like others, offering his knowledge and sound advice. His staff, including Rob Garratt, were happy to answer my questions and provide copies of documents and photographs.

Others I would like to thank especially for friendly responses to my questions and for the provision of information include Tess Egan, Library

Manager, Australian Antarctic Division, in Hobart, and Don Braben, Honorary Curator, Queensland Maritime Museum, Brisbane. Thanks too to David Jones, also of the Queensland Maritime Museum, for allowing me to quote from his article published in *Bow2Stern* in 2011 and to use a photograph taken by his late brother, Colin Jones.

Thanks to those who gave help in a variety of ways including: Lisa Ryan, at the Gympie Regional Library, for images of the wreck of the *Natone*; Margaret Mortimer for her magnificent view of Whaler's Bay; Alan Capp and Val Jessop for reading drafts; and, for answering questions, Greg Mortimer, Captain J.O. Morrice RAN Retd and Vice Admiral Peter Jones, Adjunct Professor with the Naval Studies Group, UNSW Canberra, and Commodore John Compton, RAN Retd. The following pointed a way forward when my searching hit a dead end: Lieutenant Commander Shane Monaghan, RAN, Staff Officer Hydrography, Meteorology and Oceanography Australian Hydrographic Office; Dr Michael White, OAM, QC, Adjunct Professor, Maritime and Shipping Law Unit, The University of Queensland, and Mr Paul Campbell of the Queensland Maritime Safety Bureau.

I received wonderful emails and phone calls from Lieutenant Kevin 'Shotgun' Slade RAN Retd, full of information, suggestions and enthusiasm. Kevin died suddenly, and unexpectedly, before this book was finished and before I had the opportunity to meet him. Thank you Kevin.

We should all be thankful for the amazing resources of the following national institutions which I have used: the Australian Archives, the Australian National Maritime Museum and the National Library of Australia, especially Trove, and the Library at the Australian Defence Force Academy.

Another very important contributor to this book also receives my very special thanks: artist (and step-daughter) Matilda Michell, for her illustrations of *Wyatt Earp*, used on the cover and title page.

To my husband, Jim, a big thank you for being there, for useful comments, your knowledge of things Antarctic, for proof reading and for looking after me!

Trish Burgess
28 March 2020

CONTENTS

Introduction
Wyatt Earp 1
   Why a book about a ship called Wyatt Earp? 1
   And why was this ship called Wyatt Earp? 4

Chapter 1
Building a legend 7
   From M/S *Fanefjord* to *Wyatt Earp* 7

Chapter 2 19
A legend in the making 19
   Wyatt Earp and the Ellsworth Expeditions 19
   Lincoln Ellsworth's First Antarctic Expedition 1933–34 19
   Lincoln Ellsworth's Second Antarctic Expedition, 1934–35 23
   Lincoln Ellsworth's Third Antarctic Expedition, 1935–36 29
   Lincoln Ellsworth's Fourth Antarctic Expedition, 1938–39 37

Chapter 3 45
War service and Sea Scouts 45
   RAFA *Wongala* 45
   HMAS *Wongala* 45
   SSTS *Wongala* 45
   HMAS *Wongala* 45
   HMAS *Wyatt Earp* 45

Chapter 4 73
HMAS Wyatt Earp 73
   'Twerp' and the first Australian National Antarctic Research Expedition   73

Chapter 5 93
Life after the ice 93
   Wongala 'the ship that won't give in' 93
   Natone 'Just a little ship but she could tell an amazing story' 93

Chapter 6 109
ASV (Antarctic Survey Vessel) Wyatt Earp 109

Bibliography 116

Wyatt Earp in the Antarctic. Artwork © Matilda Michell.

Introduction

H.M.A.S. WYATT EARP

Wyatt Earp

Why a book about a ship called Wyatt Earp?

The year 2019 marked the 100th anniversary since the launch of a solid, wooden ship built in 1918–1919 in Molde, Norway. At the time she was named M/S *Fanefjord* (*Motorskip*/Motorship). She was not built as a fishing vessel, as many have claimed, but as a useful coastal trading ship—an all-rounder! Initially carrying cargo from Norway to England, and then from England to France, she was then active trading around the European coast and as far north as Greenland. There was occasionally some fishing, particularly off Greenland in the summer of 1925, which was a notable season. *Fanefjord* was launched on 27 September 1919. A century after her launch, on 27 September 2019, the Australian Antarctic Division joined with the Norwegian Ambassador to Australia to host a luncheon in Hobart to commemorate this amazing little ship and her many legacies.

In 1933, after an uneventful career as a merchant vessel, she caught the eye of the Australian explorer, Sir Hubert Wilkins. He was searching for a suitable ship on behalf of the wealthy American Lincoln Ellsworth. Wilkins had already been part of expeditions and flights in both the Arctic and Antarctic. Ellsworth, too, had been involved in several Arctic journeys and now had grand plans for Antarctic voyages of exploration and Antarctic aviation feats never before achieved.

M/S *Fanefjord*, named M/V *Wyatt Earp* (Motor Vessel) by her new owner, went on to travel as far from her home port of Ålesund as was possible, making five trips to the Antarctic, four with Lincoln Ellsworth and Hubert

Wilkins between 1933 and 1939 and one for the newly formed Australian National Antarctic Research Expedition in 1948–1949.

As well as commemorating the centenary of her launching in Norway, the Hobart gathering also recalled that on 24 January 1959, nearly 40 years after she was launched and 60 years before the centenary event, the ship grounded on a stormy night, on a normally warm and sunny Queensland beach, never to sail again. It was to be her grave.

During her adventurous life she had eight names, or variations of names, in the following order: M/S *Fanefjord*, M/V *Wyatt Earp*, RAFA *Wongala* (Royal Australian Fleet Auxiliary), HMAS *Wongala*, SSTS *Wongala* (Sea Scout Training Ship), HMAS *Wyatt Earp* (His/Her Majesty's Australian Ship), *Wongala* (without any prefix) and lastly, *Natone*. This books tells her history under these names.

The construction and launch of the ship, which began her life as *Fanefjord*, is covered in Chapter 1. This chapter outlines her early years until purchased by Lincoln Ellsworth in 1933 and renamed *Wyatt Earp*. Chapter 2 tells of the four Antarctic voyages, between 1933 and 1939, made by Ellsworth and Wilkins, and Ellsworth's quest, eventually successful, to fly across the Antarctic continent.

Following the sale of the ship by Ellsworth to the Australian Government, her roles with the Department of Defence and the Royal Australian Navy (RAN) from 1939 to 1947 are chronicled in Chapter 3. As RAFA *Wongala*, and then HMAS *Wongala*, she was commissioned into the RAN for wartime duties. She was paid off in July 1944, to an uncertain future. Six months later she was lent to the South Australian Boy Scouts. She became SSTS *Wongala* on 3 March 1945. In February 1947, again as HMAS *Wongala*, she was returned to commissioned naval service, to be refitted and then used by the RAN and the Australian Antarctic Division, Department of External Affairs, for the first ANARE (Australian National Antarctic Research Expedition). In preparation for the Antarctic voyage her name was changed, yet again, to HMAS *Wyatt Earp*. This was a name the Director of Planning in Navy Office considered 'Internationally famous in polar circles'[1] given the much publicised voyages she had made with Ellsworth, as *Wyatt Earp*. She was recommissioned as HMAS *Wyatt Earp* on 17 November 1947.

Introduction

Chapter 4 contains an account of the first Australian National Antarctic Research Expedition, mainly based on the reports and diaries of the Captain and the First Lieutenant of HMAS *Wyatt Earp*, and the Chief Scientific Officer and the Executive Officer of ANARE. HMAS *Wyatt Earp* had been almost completely rebuilt at Port Adelaide. Plagued by various design troubles and delays by dockyard workers, after two false starts, HMAS *Wyatt Earp* finally left Melbourne on the ANARE voyage on 8 February 1948. After a less than successful trip, but one from which much was probably learned, she returned to Melbourne on 1 April 1948. HMAS *Wyatt Earp* was then deemed unsuitable to travel south again and was paid off in June 1948. For three years she lay alongside the wharf at Williamstown Naval Dockyard in Melbourne.

She was sold in November 1951, to the Arga Shipping Company of St Helens, Tasmania, a story retold in Chapter 5. By July 1952, she had been renamed *Wongala* and began another life as a coastal steamer carrying explosives to Western Australia and Papua, and cargo such as cement, potatoes and iron along the eastern and southern coasts of Australia. The Sydney-Ulverstone Shipping Company bought *Wongala* in 1956 for trading along the Queensland coast. With her name changed to *Natone*, she had entered the last phase of her life. As *Natone* she sailed to Fiji, Papua-New Guinea, Lord Howe Island and along the east coast from Tasmania to Cairns with various cargoes, including cattle.

In January 1959, after battling cyclonic weather during a passage south along the Queensland coast from Lae, she developed leaks that her crew could not contain. The engine room flooded, her sails were hoisted and *Natone* searched for shelter. During the night she ran aground near Mudlo Rocks, 110 miles north of Brisbane. She was lost.

Chapter 6, an epilogue, is about a relatively new vessel, one also bearing the famous name. Although the 'original' ship was wrecked, a new *Wyatt Earp* joined the Australian Hydrographic Service in 1993. ASV *Wyatt Earp* (Antarctic Survey Vessel) has since joined the fleet of Antarctic heroes!

Much has been written, by many people, over the years about the world-wide voyages of this little ship. This book brings all her various histories together.

And why was this ship called Wyatt Earp?

In 1933, as the new owner of *Fanefjord,* Lincoln Ellsworth changed the name of his ship to *Wyatt Earp.* Why use the name of the legendary frontier lawman and gambler, Wyatt Berry Stapp Earp (born in 1848) who is perhaps most famous for his role in the gunfight at the O.K. Corral in Tombstone? In 1881, when this took place, Wyatt was working as a bank security guard. His brother, Virgil, was town Marshal and brother Morgan, along with another legend, 'Doc' Holliday, were the face of law and order. They confronted a group of cowboys (also known as thieves, murderers and cattle rustlers) in a gun fight which left three cowboys dead and two on the run. Morgan and Virgil Earp and Holliday were wounded. The three Earps and Holliday were charged with murder but later found not guilty. Since then, the gunfight has been the subject of several films.

Wyatt Earp was neither a saint nor hero. He was variously a professional gambler, who owned several saloons and at least one brothel, mined for silver and gold, raced horses and refereed boxing matches. The latter led to trouble when he called a foul and many thought he had fixed the fight! He moved frequently, at one time following another brother, James, to Dodge City, where he became an assistant city Marshal. He made a good deal of money in the Alaska and Nevada gold rushes by owning liquor licences and saloons.

> Wyatt Earp might have passed into oblivion, along with the gunfight that is synonymous with his name, were it not for novelist Stuart N. Lake. During the 1920s Lake interviewed and wrote about another Old West gunfighter, William 'Bat' Masterson, who continually spoke about the bravest man he ever knew, Wyatt Earp. Wanting to record as much Western folklore as he could, Lake sought out Earp and asked to write his biography. Earp agreed and Lake conducted a series of interviews.[2]

Before the book was published Wyatt Earp died at his home, on 13 January 1929, aged 80. *Wyatt Earp: Frontier Marshal,* published in October 1931 'glorified not only Earp, but also the Old West in a way that no one had glorified it before'[3]. The book became a bestseller in America during the Depression, raising Earp to folk hero status. Lincoln Ellsworth, despite all his money, needed heroes. He remarked:

> The vessel I christened *Wyatt Earp* after the famous frontier marshal of the West. On this, my own expedition, I could indulge every whim and fancy that did not interfere with its efficiency, and one of my whims was to imbue the whole enterprise with the spirit of Wyatt Earp, the bravest man I ever heard of.
>
> I am frankly a hero-worshiper and a sentimentalist. For years I have made almost a cult of the memory of Wyatt Earp. I have spent much time collecting every souvenir and trinket I could find associated with that unbelievably brave man. Only the other day I secured, after a three year effort, the hair-trigger six-shooter with which he fought his famous battle with Ike Clanton's gang. I hang this gun in its holster over my bedpost, wherever I may be, and I expect to keep up this custom to the end of my life.
>
> I don't suppose any vessel ever sailed before so filled with presence of the figure whose name it bore as was the Wyatt Earp when it set out for the Antarctic. In the ship's library were two books about Earp: *Wyatt Earp, Frontier Marshal*, by Stuart N. Lake, and *Tombstone*, by Walter Noble Burns, author also of Wilkins's favourite American book, *The Saga of Billy the Kid*. Everybody on board read these two volumes, the Norwegians who understood English translating it to those who didn't. Most of them had never heard of Earp before the voyage.
>
> In my cabin hung Wyatt Earp's cartridge belt. When I made the flight at last, I had this historic trophy on the Polar Star.[4]

Ellsworth had earlier written:

> It may sound paradoxical, but were I to name my real heroes they would be taken from the ranks of those great pioneers and not from the roster of explorers. And were I to single out the greatest of them all, I would mention Wyatt Earp, the man after whom I named that sturdy and reliable little boat which took me on my travels to Antarctica.[5]

Endnotes

1. Minute dated 9 June 1947, from Director of Planning to DCNS (Deputy Chief of Naval Staff) and 2NM (Second Naval Member). Document from Wyatt Earp File, Naval History Section – Sea Power Centre.
2. Jeff Maynard, *Antarctica's Lost Aviator*, Pegasus Books, 2019, pp. 70–71.
3. Jeff Maynard, *Antarctica's Lost Aviator*, Pegasus Books, 2019, p. 71.
4. Lincoln Ellsworth, *Beyond Horizons*, Doubleday, Doran & Company, Inc., 1938. p. 254–255.
5. Lincoln Ellsworth, *Exploring Today*, Dodd, Mead & Company, 1935, p. 26.

Chapter 1

Building a legend

From M/S *Fanefjord* to *Wyatt Earp*

It is 1919. The Great War is over. The Depression is yet to come and, in Norway, neutral during the War and affected less than some European countries, the fishing fleets are trying to meet the increasing demand for food throughout Europe. Norway's seas are brimming with herring. Norway has the longest coastline in Europe. In the small town of Molde, on the Moldefjord, as in similar centres along the coast, new ships are being built to replace many lost during the War, and for the rapidly expanding fishing fleets. Norway's economic future looks good with recovery of the merchant and fishing fleets and vast supplies of fish available to be caught. In the period between the World Wars, Norway's traditional fishing, sealing and hunting activities were all expanding rapidly, particularly in the Arctic.

On 27 September 1919, coming off the slipway of Bolsønes shipyard, in Molde, was a small cargo ship built for work in icy waters. She was constructed from Norwegian pine and oak. Building boats in wood was the expertise of Bolsønes shipyard and, immediately after the Great War, there was a shortage of steel.[1] Her beams and planks gave a total thickness of 19 in.[2] This ship was named *Fanefjord*, after the 20 km long fjord east of Molde. She went on to travel as far away from her home port of Ålesund as it is possible to do, making five voyages to the Antarctic, four with American Lincoln Ellsworth and Australian Hubert Wilkins and another for the Australian National Antarctic Research Expedition. And nearly forty years later, on 24 January 1959, she was wrecked during a storm on what was usually a warm and sunny Queensland beach!

(R.Fot.77078) One of the plans of *Fanefjord*. Courtesy: Romsdalsmuseet, Norway.

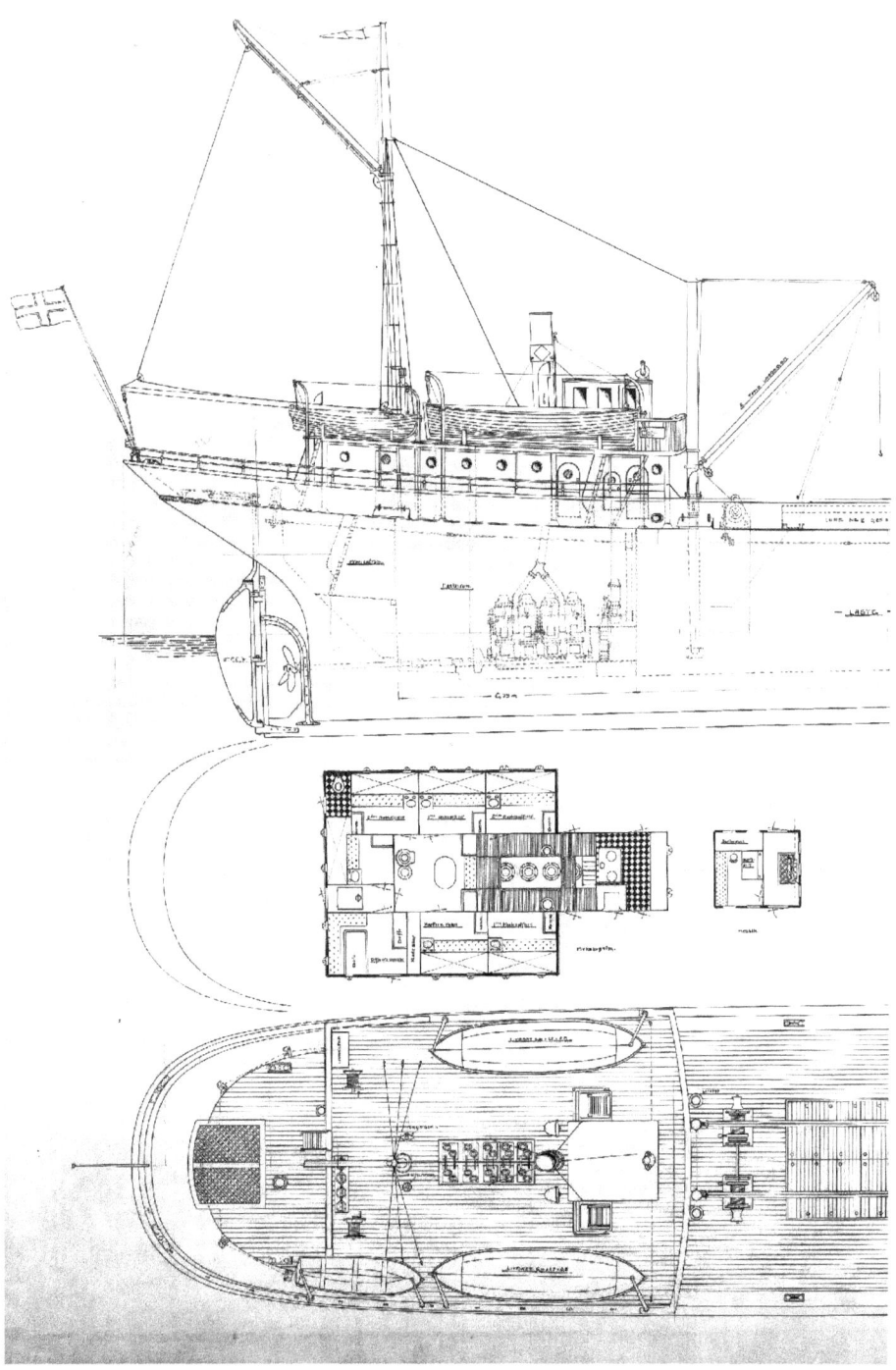

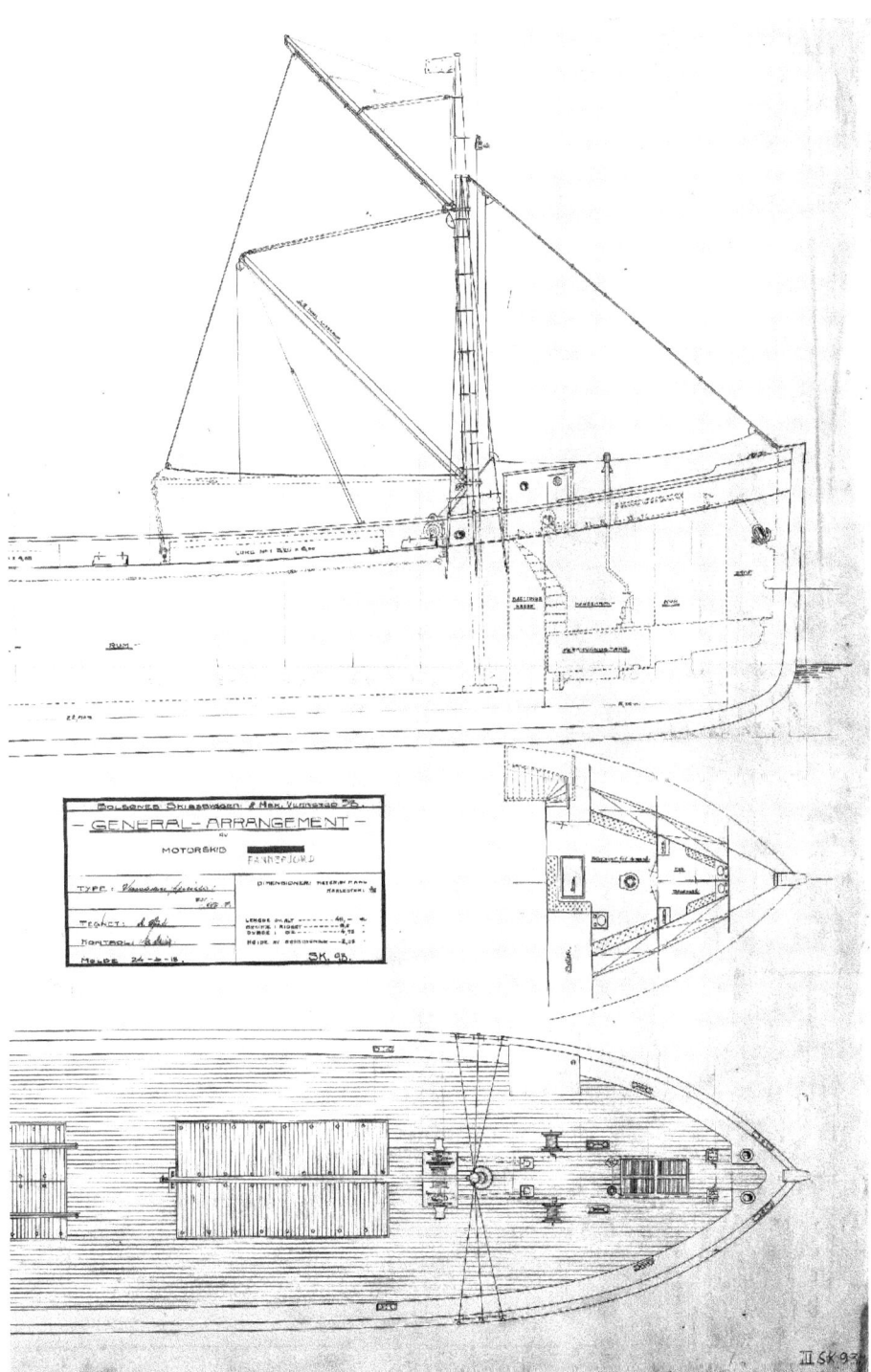

(R.Fot.75727) Building *Fanefjord* at Bolsønes Shipyard in Molde, Norway, 1918. Courtesy: Romsdalsmuseet, Norway.

Fanefjord was one of the two largest ships built in the Bolsønes shipyard, which would go on building ships until 1984. 'The ship wasn't built as a fishing ship in general, but was used as a fishing ship during the big fishing season at Greenland in the summer of 1925. The ship had also been used for fishing for several occasions before and later as well.'[3] *Fanefjord* was built for Edv. Christensen of Fanefjords Rederi A/S[4] of Molde. Two days after being launched, on 29 September 1919, *Fanefjord* sailed to Trondheim to load 'props', either timber marine props for English coal mines or propellers from the Trondheim Mechanical Workshop, one of the largest in Norway. British newspaper archives show that *Fanefjord* arrived in Hartlepool, a small port on England's north-east coast, on 29 October 1919. She sailed again on 10 November for Goole, on the River Ouse, 50 miles inland from the North Sea in Yorkshire. She brought more 'props' to England in August 1920, and then made several voyages between England and Denmark and Norway. In 1923, 1924 and 1927 she visited several English ports and in 1931 again coming from Trondheim, she loaded timber in Wales. In December 1931 and January, February, and May 1932 she brought potatoes to England from Trondheim, often returning to Ålesund and Molde with coke or coal. *Fanefjord* also worked on charter to Iceland, France and other European countries.

Technical details tell us she was

> 400 tons with a 15-foot draft. The 135-foot craft was built in 1919, at Molde, of Norwegian pine and oak. She had a single deck and was powered by a semi-diesel engine capable of driving the ship at a speed of seven to eight knots. Later fitted with auxiliary sails [sic[5]], the vessel was capable of nine knots under a favouring wind.[6]

Between her first voyage in 1919 and August 1933 Fanefjord had a number of owners and in 1930 she had a new engine fitted: a Bolinder BHK 320, NKH 89, Speed: 10 knots:

SEPTEMBER 1919	Fanefjords Shipowners A/S (Edv. Christensen), Molde
JULY 1923	Roalds Sønner A/S, Ålesund
c.1925	Roalds Sønner (Elias Roald, Ålesund)
MARCH 1926	Johs Paulsen, Ålesund
MARCH 1927	A/S M/S Fanefjord (Harald Paulsen) Ålesund
JULY 1932	Axel Holm, Ålesund
AUGUST 1933	Wyatt Earp A/S Ltd (Axel Holm) Ålesund[7]

Fanefjord spent nearly fourteen years as a tough and sturdy workhorse carrying cargoes for six different owners in the icy cold and rough seas she and her crews knew well. By the 1930s the 'Heroic Age' of Arctic and Antarctic exploration had ended.

Aeroplanes and ships better suited to the tasks asked of them as well as mechanical vehicles to support the expeditions into the huge still unexplored polar areas became more readily available. At that time, in America, there was a very wealthy and very adventurous man, Lincoln Ellsworth. Born in 1880, he (and his father) financed and co-led the first trans-Arctic air crossing, the Amundsen-Ellsworth Airship Expedition in 1926, and the first Trans-Antarctic flight in 1935. When Ellsworth was 23 he worked for five years in Canada as a surveyor and engineer, never gaining formal qualifications, followed by three years with the US Biological Survey. In 1917 he joined the United States Army and travelled to France, hoping to be trained as a pilot. In his autobiography, *Beyond Horizons*, he states that he learned to fly in France during the War. 'A Franco-American flying unit began training at Tours on the Loire, southwest of Paris.' He was told he was too old to train as a pilot but was taken on to become an observer but after some confusion at the airfield, 'the French instructors set about training me to pilot an airplane'. They trained in old Caudron biplanes and he received his élève pilots' insignia and later was promoted to sergeant[8]. He was 'assigned to clerical work, before a bout of influenza caused him to be sent home.'[9]

(R.Fot.75729) The launch of *Fanefjord*, sea trials and delivery from the shipyard. Taken at Bolsønes Shipyard, Molde, 27 September 1919. Courtesy: Romsdalsmuseet, Norway.

Ellsworth led a wandering life with no real goals but his experiences in France, including meeting Roald Amundsen, the famous Norwegian explorer, would stand him in good stead in years to come. Family money and the lure of aerial Arctic exploration fired his imagination and his enthusiasm and he persuaded his father to support Amundsen financially in the first (unsuccessful) polar flight, which started on 21 May 1925. It took much more persuasion for his father to allow Lincoln to join Amundsen and four other men in two Dornier flying boats, to fly to the North Pole. In 1926 he and Amundsen were joined by Italian Umberto Nobile and, leaving from Spitsbergen, they flew to Alaska (5,463 km) in the airship *Norge*, the first aircraft to overfly the Arctic. Then Ellsworth began his wandering again, wishing for an expedition he could lead but one that he did not have to organise!

So many 'firsts' were waiting to be accomplished. United States Navy, Admiral Richard Byrd, pioneer aviator and polar explorer, flew non-stop across the Atlantic in 1927, only just beaten by Charles Lindbergh, and, in 1928, another polar explorer, the Australian Hubert Wilkins, and his co-pilot, Carl Ben Eielson, flew from Alaska to Spitsbergen. In the Antarctic summer of 1928–29 Wilkins explored the coast of Graham Land as part of the British Imperial Antarctic Expedition, as deputy to Dr John Cope: a rather unsuccessful event with big ideas and high hopes not realised but experience gained. That same summer Admiral Byrd was in the Antarctic, setting up his base camp, 'Little America',[10] on the iceshelf beside the Bay of Whales in the Ross Sea. 'Little America' would become vitally important to Lincoln Ellsworth's survival in 1935–36. At the end of 1929, Byrd, pilot Bernt Balchen and two others became the first to fly to the South Pole and back.

Wilkins's extensive experience in Arctic and Antarctic 'adventures' explains why he was so extraordinarily useful to Lincoln Ellsworth and, thus, his lengthy involvement with *Wyatt Earp*. He was born George Hubert Wilkins in Netfield, near Mount Bryan East, in outback South Australia in 1888. He grew up on his parents' property, attending a local, one-teacher school, to become a 'war correspondent and photographer, polar explorer, naturalist, geographer, climatologist and aviator'.[11] He studied electrical engineering in Adelaide before an interest in photography and cinematography led him abroad in 1908. He learned to fly in England in 1912 and, as a war correspondent, reported fighting between the Turks and Bulgarians that year.

In 1913–16 he was deputy leader on Vilhjalmur Stefansson's Canadian Arctic expedition, learning much about survival in polar regions from the Indigenous people. Wilkins had a lifelong passion for establishing permanent bases in the Arctic and Antarctic to improve weather forecasting. In London, through Lady Kathleen Scott, widow of 'Scott of the Antarctic', Wilkins met Frank Hurley, the Australian photographer on both Mawson's 1911 and Shackleton's 1914 Antarctic expeditions.[12] Wilkins returned to Australia in 1917 and was commissioned into the Australian Imperial Force

(Australian Flying Corps), serving on the Western Front and in 1918 as official photographer. He met Captain Frank Hurley again and later they worked together in the Australian War Records office with Charles Bean. Wilkins was awarded the Military Cross and later a Bar to his MC. In 1919 he joined Charles Bean 'to reconstruct Australia's part in the Gallipoli Peninsula campaign'. Later that year his plane in the England to Australia air race crashed in Crete. He returned to Australia by sea, leaving the AIF in September.

Wilkins first visited Antarctica in 1920–21 with the British Imperial Antarctic Expedition, exploring the coast of Graham Land and calling at Deception Island and Paradise Harbour, an experience that would prove useful later. Sir Ernest Shackleton invited him to join his 1921–22 expedition on the *Quest*; the voyage, in fact, on which Shackleton died while the ship was in harbour at Grytviken, South Georgia, and where he is buried. The expedition continued after Shackleton's death at the request of Lady Shackleton but, in Wilkins's words, 'We accomplished little on an expedition that ran six times over budget. ... We were forced to abandon our dreams when the ice in the Weddell Sea proved too much for our defective vessel and accept failure before making the long trip home to England'.[13]

In 1925 Wilkins conceived a project to fly across the Arctic, but lack of funds and the unsuitability of the Fokker aircraft he bought meant the idea had to be postponed. In 1927, taking off from Point Barrow in Alaska, he made another attempt, again unsuccessfully. Finally, in April 1928, with Carl Ben Eielson as pilot, he flew from Point Barrow, Alaska, over the Arctic Sea to Spitsbergen (Svalbard) in Norway. King George V knighted Sir Hubert Wilkins in June 'for his gallant war service, his contributions to the natural sciences, and his polar service'[14]. Following this achievement, Wilkins was offered financial sponsorship by the US media mogul, William Randolph Hearst, in return for exclusive rights to his expeditions for aerial exploration of the Antarctic in the southern summer of 1928–29. In August 1929 he was part of the Hearst-sponsored, 21 day, around-the-world flight of the airship *Graf Zepplin*. Wilkins followed this with plans to take a surplus US Navy submarine, *Nautilus*, under the pack ice to the North Pole, but the planning and preparation was dogged by mechanical problems and lack of finance. And then Sir Hubert Wilkins encountered Lincoln Ellsworth!

They met in Switzerland, in the spring of 1930, instantly finding common interests. Ellsworth agreed to support Wilkins's plans financially. With more than US$70,000 he backed the now officially named Wilkins-Ellsworth Trans-Arctic Expedition. A submarine dive under the North Pole, it was ultimately unsuccessful.

Ellsworth also shared his ideas for an Antarctic expedition. When Wilkins returned to New York the pair studied a map of Antarctica. Ellsworth wanted to make a flight from Byrd's 'Little America' base in the Ross Sea to the head of the Weddell Sea and return, thus becoming the first to make a trans-Antarctic flight. Wilkins agreed to take charge of the project, including finding the right men and equipment, the support needed and a suitable ship to provide the ship-based support.

Wilkins had visited Norway on several occasions and in 1933 he went there again—to find a wooden vessel to become their expedition ship. He found *Fanefjord*. The ship was available, purchased and, over two months, refitted. 'The ship was modernised in Bolsønes Verft (Bolsønes Shipyard), Liaaen Verft (Shipyard) and some few last hour adds in Bergen at Marineholmen.'[15] The accommodation was rebuilt, the rigging moved and metal sheathing and oak planking fitted from the stem of amidships to withstand the Antarctic pack ice. She was also given a fore and an aft rig of Marconi-type sails, extra fuel and water tanks were also installed.[16] The most detailed description of the work done comes from an article published in a New Zealand newspaper which stated 'that she is better equipped for the expedition's purpose than any vessel preceding her to the Antarctic'. It outlined what had been done to the ship:

> Ten great steel tanks are bedded on her keelson, and six others are held to her decks with massive angle irons. These tanks will carry fresh water and fuel to serve her engines for a journey of 10,000 miles or more, without refueling. Four curved tanks conforming to the shapely hull house 20 tons of fresh water—enough to last the 16 souls on board for several months.
>
> Above the forward tanks and between the oak-sheathed bows is a spacious forecastle fitted with nine bunks. Each bunk is equipped with individual electric light and heating—equipment needed not

alone for comfort but also to save the risk of fire, which might be started if oil lamps were used.

Catwalk below decks

Thickly built wooden vessels as a rule—and this ship is no exception—stay well on top of the water in heavy seas and few waves come aboard. But in the roaring forties and raging fifties the crew will suffer many a ducking. To serve health and comfort a catwalk has been arranged below decks from the forecastle through the hold and engine room to the bridge deck and messroom. In rough weather the sails will at least be able to start their watch in dry clothing.

The bridge of the boat is well aft and above the engines, and along each side of the poop are the officers' cabins, the mess room and the wireless room, the bathroom and photographic darkroom. The small mess room is set up in one of the starboard cabins and will seat seven men at a sitting. The bathroom on this ship is not as the bathroom on many expeditions—a place where odds and ends are piled until they reach the ceiling, but a modern lavatory with hot and cold water always at the tap, a shower bath and bath tub. Cleanliness may be next to godliness in temperate latitudes, but so far as history records it has been next to nothing on many polar expeditions.[17]

Ellsworth renamed the ship *Wyatt Earp*, after the legendary marshal and his childhood hero whom he greatly admired. The ship was registered *Wyatt Earp*, on 26 June 1933, after passing formal inspection at Ålesund, Norway.

Ellsworth kept his private finances separate from those of the expedition For the registration of the ship he formed a Norwegian company, Wyatt Earp A/S Ltd. Ten thousand shares at one kroner per share were issued with Aksel Holm, a local shipping agent holding 6,000 shares, Ellsworth 3,000 shares and Wilkins 1,000 shares.[18]

Having ensured he would protect his business interests, Ellsworth needed to ensure he also protected his place in history books. While the *Wyatt Earp* was still in Norway, every member of the crew, including Wilkins and Balchen, signed an agreement that stipulated they would not make any broadcasts, grant any interviews, distribute any photographs, or write any articles without Ellsworth's consent. Wilkins signed an additional agreement that he would write, 'detailed articles while on the vessel *Wyatt Earp*; said articles to appear only under the name Lincoln Ellsworth.'[19]

There were further conditions and restrictions.

The plane, *Polar Star*, was loaded on the ship in Bergen and on 29 July 1933, two days after the agreements were signed, and, under her new name, *Wyatt Earp* sailed from Bergen for the Antarctic, commanded by Captain Baard Holth. Her course was the Canary Islands, Cape Town, South Africa, and Dunedin, New Zealand. Along with Captain Holth, the eight officers and crewmen were all Arctic or Antarctic veterans, having been members of Norwegian whaling voyages. There were 17 expedition members, including Ellsworth and Wilkins, and Bernt Balchen, the pilot, who had previously flown with Byrd. Included on board were a doctor, meteorologist, radio operator and mechanic.

Ellsworth's first Antarctic expedition was under way.

(78207) *Fanefjord/Wyatt Earp*, Bergen, July 1933. Courtesy: Magnus Johannessen's photo album, Romsdalsmuseet, Norway.

Endnotes

1. Personal email from Kenneth Staurest Fåne, Conservator, Romsdalsmuseet, Norway. 11 November 2019.
2. 'The Wyatt Earp. Ellsworth's Ship', *Auckland Star*, 15 August 1933. From the digitised version https://paperspast.natlib.govt.nz/newspapers/AS19330815.2.37.
3. Personal email from Kenneth Staurest Fåne, Conservator, Romsdalsmuseet, Norway. 11 November 2019.
4. A/S means *Aksjeselskap*, a Norwegian business that has a minimum level of funding and limited liability, with a Norwegian national holding the majority of shares.
5. 'Fanefjord had sails from the start. It was built with sails and motor.' Personal email from Kenneth Staurest Fåne, Conservator, Romsdalsmuseet, Norway. 11 November 2019.
6. Kenneth J. Bertrand,' Ellsworth's Transantarctic Flight, 1935', in *Americans in Antarctica 1775–1948*, American Geographical Society Special Publication No.39, 1971, p. 363.
7. www.Sjohistorie.no/en/skip/320622/
8. Lincoln Ellsworth, *Beyond Horizons*, Doubleday, Doran & Company, Inc., 1938, pp. 102–105.
9. Jeff Maynard, *Antarctica's Lost Aviator*, Pegasus Books, 2019, p. 8.
10. There have been five bases called 'Little America' on or close to the original site, on the Ross Ice Shelf. All have been lost into the sea over the years.
11. R.A.Swan, 'Wilkins, Sir George Hubert (1888–1958)', *Australian Dictionary of Biography*, National Centre of Biography, Australian National University, http://abd.anu.edu.au./biography/wilkins-sir-george-hubert-9099/text16045, published first in hardcopy 1990, accessed online 5 February 2020.
12. A.F. Pike, 'Hurley, James Francis (Frank) (1885–1962)', *Australian Dictionary of Biography*, National Centre of Biography, Australian National University, http://adb.anu.edu.au/biography/hurley-james-francis-frank-6774/test1715, published first in hardcopy 1983, accessed online 3 February 2020.
13. Malcolm Andrews, *Hubert Who?* ABC Books and HarperCollins Publisher, 2011, p. 118.
14. Encyclopedia Arctic 15-volume unpublished reference work (1947–51) Sir Hubert Wilkins Dartmouth College Library https://collections.dartmouth.edu/arctica-beta/html/EA15-77.html
15. Personal email from Kenneth Staurest Fåne, Conservator, Romsdalsmuseet, Norway. 11 November 2019.
16. 'Ellsworth's Transantarctic Flight' in *Americans in Antarctica 1777–1948*, p. 363.
17. 'The Wyatt Earp. Ellsworth's Ship', *Auckland Star*, 15 August 1933. From the digitised version https://paperspast.natlib.govt.nz/newspapers/AS19330815.2.37.
18. Jeff Maynard, *Antarctica's Lost Aviator*, Pegasus Books, 2019, p. 84.
19. Jeff Maynard, *Antarctica's Lost Aviator*, Pegasus Books, 2019, p. 84.

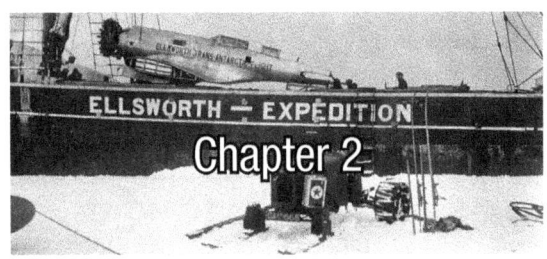

Chapter 2

A legend in the making

Wyatt Earp and the Ellsworth Expeditions

Lincoln Ellsworth's First Antarctic Expedition 1933–34

What the ice did to the plane!

Lincoln Ellsworth wanted to be the first person to fly across the Antarctic. Sir Hubert Wilkins was already the first person to make a flight in the Antarctic. In December 1928 Wilkins, and co-pilot Ben Eielson, had taken off from and returned to Deception Island, flying 1,200 miles in ten hours. The plan for the Ellsworth Expedition was to sail *Wyatt Earp* to the Bay of Whales, in the Ross Sea, and unload the plane, *Polar Star*, on to suitable ice. The plane would then take off and fly across the Antarctic to the Weddell Sea, and return to the Ross Sea where *Wyatt Earp* would be waiting.

From Bergen, Norway, on 29 July 1933, under the command of Captain Baard Holth, *Wyatt Earp* sailed without Lincoln Ellsworth! He joined his ship in Dunedin, New Zealand. A large crowd gathered on the wharf to farewell *Wyatt Earp* and many small boats followed her down the harbour.

In open sea, the *Wyatt Earp* was hit by a gale that lasted two days. It pitched and rolled, as it was prone to do, but otherwise proved seaworthy. Wilkins wrote to his wife, 'The ship rolls a great deal but it is not a viscous [sic vicious?] crazy roll, just swaying from side to side. We get used to it.'[1]

The ship called at ports normal for such a voyage at that time:

The Wyatt Earp entered Las Palmas in the Canary Islands at 6:30 AM, on Sunday, August 13, 1933, and sailed again at 7:45 PM on Monday, August 14th. She arrived at Cape Town on Tuesday, September 19th, and left there, headed for Dunedin, on Thursday, September 28th. The ship arrived at Dunedin on Friday, November 10th, and sailed for the Bay of Whales in Antarctica on Tuesday, December 5, 1933. The Wyatt Earp entered in the Bay of Whales at mid-day on Sunday, January 7, 1934.[2]

Wyatt Earp reached the pack ice one week after leaving Dunedin. The ice was heavy, closing off access to the Ross Sea. In a 'Special' to the *Daily News* in Perth Mr Lincoln Ellsworth messaged, and reported under big headlines:

(78216) Bernt Balchen (pilot), Lincoln Ellsworth and Sir Hubert Wilkins in Dunedin, New Zealand, 1933, at the start of the First Expedition. Courtesy: Magnus Johannessen's photo album, Romsdalsmuseet, Norway.

ELLSWORTH'S SHIP CAUGHT IN PACK ICE—Wyatt Earp Two Hundred Miles from Open Sea:

AT SEA. Dec. 17. We are about 200 miles inside the great Polar ice-pack, held up by wide, heavy floes. Snow is driving up with a south-west wind and the whole pack is in motion. To be locked in there without means of propulsion would be a serious affair, but we expect that the wind and current will soon make rifts in the ice and leave lanes of open water, of which we may take advantage and proceed.

Our entry into the pack was sudden and dramatic: our only warning was a quick drop in the temperature to two degrees below freezing, and a light fog. Three hours later two huge icebergs loomed in sight, one to port and one to starboard. Fitting guardians they seem to the realm of the ice king.

We passed between them, and two hours later, and 180 miles to the north of where Rear-Admiral Byrd found it in 1930, we entered the Polar pack, a world apart from the one we left, and where silence and desolation reign supreme. Lifeless and unfriendly it may seem, yet it holds a fascination all its own.[3]

For 22 days *Wyatt Earp* tried to find a way through the ice:

> For 13 days of the 22 days they were locked in the ice at a total standstill. Much of the time was spent forging ahead to collide with the ice, backing up and then ramming ahead again. In the process, the gears were worn down to the point where their half-speed was entirely lost.[4]

The voyage had taken over five months! Their stay at the Bay of Whales was short-lived—ten days in fact. *Wyatt Earp* moored to the edge of the ice and the plane, *Polar Star*, on board since Norway, was brought out of the hold, had her wings attached (which took two days) and the oiled paper wrapping, to prevent corrosion, was removed. It was lowered by crane on to level snow. By 10 January, the Northrop 'Gamma 2B' plane was ready for testing and Balchen and Ellsworth took it on three short flights. All went well and *Polar Star* was moved closer to the shore, still on the ice, as there were heavy seas at the edge.

About 4 o'clock in the morning shouts from the men on watch caused everyone to run up on deck where they witnessed heavy swells and a grinding mass of ice cakes and floes for five miles inland. Off in the distance, stranded on a small cake, was the *Polar Star*. It wasn't long before the small ice-cake broke in half, dropping the skis and fuselage into a crevasse with only the wings supporting the plane above the bay.[5]

When the men managed to drag *Polar Star* back on board *Wyatt Earp* it was clear it was badly damaged. The skis were cracked and one wing was bent—clearly a job for the factory in California.

Wyatt Earp left the Bay of Whales on 17 January, and returned to Dunedin on 28 January 1934. *Polar Star* was sent back to the United States and to the Northrop factory on the tanker *Texaco South Africa*. *Wyatt Earp* remained in Dunedin for maintenance until August. Additional repairs were needed due to damage when berthing. As noted earlier she had no half-speed and hit the dock damaging the bow. In February 1934, Ellsworth returned to the United States, to San Francisco, on the luxury ocean liner, SS *Mariposa*.[6] His wife met him there and they crossed the country to New York by train before going to Europe by sea. They spent five months at Lenzburg Castle in Switzerland which he had inherited from his father.

(78293) Unloading *Polar Star* in the Bay of Whales, 1934. Courtesy: Magnus Johannessen's photo album, Romsdalsmuseet, Norway.

(78267) Alongside the ice, *Polar Star* assembled and unloaded, in the Bay of Whales, 1934. Courtesy: Magnus Johannessen's photo album, Romsdalsmuseet, Norway.

(78296) The damaged *Polar Star,* Bay of Whales, January 1934. Courtesy: Magnus Johannessen's photo album, Romsdalsmuseet, Norway.

Lincoln Ellsworth's Second Antarctic Expedition, 1934–35

'Defeat by the weather I could accept . . .'

Plans for Ellsworth's second Antarctic expedition had to be altered, given the problems of the previous trip. There was a change in the flight plan to a one-way flight. Instead of flying from the Ross Sea to the Weddell Sea and return, it was decided that *Wyatt Earp* would leave the plane and crew on an island somewhere along the Antarctic peninsula and that the ship would then sail to the Bay of Whales and meet the fliers there. Deception Island was chosen as a suitable island. Wilkins was familiar with the area,

(78237) Unloading *Polar Star* in Dunedin, New Zealand, after the accident on the First Expedition, 1934. Courtesy: Magnus Johannessen's photo album, Romsdalsmuseet, Norway.

having arrived there on 24 December 1920 on one of Lars Christensen's ships as part of an unsuccessful expedition headed by Dr John Cope. On a later trip Wilkins became the first person to make a short flight in the Antarctic, on 16 November 1928, in the vicinity of Deception Island, and a much longer flight of 1,200 miles on 20 December 1928.[7]

For Ellsworth's expedition, Wilkins thought that it might be possible to fly across the Antarctic from Deception Island to 'Little America', on the Bay of Whales in the Ross Sea, where they had been early that year. It was a shorter route than the previous plan, so required less fuel. This in turn would allow them to carry extra supplies—a sledge, tent, more food and camping equipment.

After repairs in Dunedin, *Wyatt Earp* sailed to Auckland in August, to load the repaired *Polar Star*, returned from the factory in America. Later *Wyatt Earp* visited Wellington to load scientific equipment and embark Sir Hubert Wilkins. She returned to Dunedin where Ellsworth joined her and sailed on 19 September 1934, still chasing Ellsworth's dream to be the first to fly across the Antarctic—but this time from the Weddell Sea to the

Ross Sea. Ellsworth was Leader, and Wilkins, the Manager and Technical Assistant. Bernt Balchen was again the pilot and the party included the doctor, radio operator, meteorologist and mechanic along with nine Norwegian crew again commanded by Captain Holth.

(78325) *Wyatt Earp* tied up at the former whaling station, Port Foster, in the harbour at Deception Island, October or November 1934. Note the steam rising from the thermal pools along the foreshore. Courtesy: Magnus Johannessen's photo album, Romsdalsmuseet, Norway.[8]

(78388) *Wyatt Earp*, at Deception Island, Christmas Eve, 24 December 1934. Courtesy: Magnus Johannessen's photo album, Romsdalsmuseet, Norway.

The 6,500 km voyage was not easy. The weather—gales, blizzards and hurricanes—was extremely wild almost every day. The voyage took twenty-six days to reach Deception Island. The ordeal was not over as the worst weather, including exceptionally low visibility, hit *Wyatt Earp* as she approached the island. Deception Harbour is a caldera, formed by an extinct volcano. There is a narrow entrance, 'Neptune's Bellows', and this was partially blocked by an iceberg. They eventually entered the harbour and arrived at the abandoned Norwegian whaling station, Port Forster, on 14 October. Next day they were frozen in for five days with more rain, sleet and high winds. Nothing could be done to start assembling *Polar Star* until the weather improved. Eventually the plane was unloaded and dragged up the steep beach. On the evening of 29 October:

> They deemed it advisable to run the Wasp engine a little and after a half-turn of the propeller, there was a terrific jar and a loud snap as the engine stalled. The engine broke a connecting rod and despite boxes of spare parts taken along, none were included though everything else was there.[9]

Organised by radio, spare rods were flown to the Chilean port of Magallanes (later Punta Arenas). Ellsworth and four others remained on Deception Island and *Wyatt Earp* left on 31 October, returning on 16 November with the required part.[10] During that time the snowfields to be used for takeoff had melted, exposing patches of rock. Ten days later the engine was repaired but the inclement weather was against them again. Fog and mild temperatures continued. On 27 November, *Polar Star* was reloaded and *Wyatt Earp* sailed south searching for another suitable area. They moored to the ice shelf at Snow Hill Island on 3 December 1934. On 18 December *Polar Star* did a short test flight and all was in readiness for departure the next morning. Overnight the weather deteriorated and the flight was postponed. A similar test flight and change of weather occurred on 31 December/1 January. On 3 January 1935 a flight of two hours and 28 minutes, with Ellsworth and Balchen as pilots, had to turn back because of weather conditions. During all the waiting time on Snow Hill Island Ellsworth managed to collect 150 specimens of 28 species of fossils. Three of the species had never been found before in the Antarctic. They were all deposited in the American Museum of Natural History.[11]

Pack ice was beginning to close in and gales and blizzards made loading *Polar Star* impossible until 9 January. Again disappointed, Ellsworth recalled his thoughts on leaving Snow Hill Island: 'Defeat by the weather I could accept philosophically and try again.'[12]

They sailed north but found the Antarctic Sound blocked with ice and had to wait in shelter for a northerly wind to clear the passage. Five days later and after some nasty experiences with wind, pack ice and cliffs, *Wyatt Earp* stopped briefly in Hope Bay before arriving back at Deception Island on 20 January. *Polar Star* was dismantled and stowed below. On 21 January, regretful, but well aware of the consequences of weather on their plans, *Wyatt Earp* sailed from Deception Island to Montevideo, Uruguay, arriving on 2 February. Here the aircraft was stored and the ship laid up. Ellsworth returned to New York by air, via Buenos Aires and the west coast of the United States.

(78223) Lincoln Ellsworth and Dr Berg gazing at the landscape at Snow Hill Island. Nordenskjöld's hut is visible down at the beach. Courtesy: Magnus Johannessen's photo album, Romsdalsmuseet, Norway.

(78374) *Polar Star* at Deception Island, 1934, amongst the whale bones.
Courtesy: Magnus Johannessen's photo album, Romsdalsmuseet, Norway.

(78265) *Wyatt Earp* alongside ice in harbour at Deception Island, 1934. Courtesy: Magnus Johannessen's photo album, Romsdalsmuseet, Norway.

Chapter 2   A legend in the making

(78394) *Wyatt Earp* alongside ice at Snow Hill Island, December 1934. Courtesy: Magnus Johannessen's photo album, Romsdalsmuseet, Norway.

Lincoln Ellsworth's Third Antarctic Expedition, 1935–36

Success and rescue ... in the Ross Sea

Before the third expedition could begin Ellsworth had to find a new pilot. Having given up two years to Antarctic exploration, Bernt Balchen resigned to return to Norway and work in commercial flying. Ellsworth found two pilots, both working for Canadian Airways, who agreed to join the expedition. Herbert Hollick-Kenyon (born in London, migrated to Canada with his parents when he was about 13), and J. H. Lymburner (from a farm in Ontario, Canada). Hollick-Kenyon joined the Canadian army as a trooper in 1914 and transferred to the Royal Flying Corps in 1917. He flew for Western Canada Airways from 1928. As a pilot he took part in several search and rescue missions for missing polar expeditions.

In May 1935 Ellsworth and his wife made their annual visit to Switzerland and then took the *Graf Zeppelin* airship to Rio de Janeiro. His wife returned to the United States and Ellsworth boarded an Italian ship, *Augustus*, to Montevideo. His ship, plane, crew and the new pilots were awaiting his arrival. On 18 October, *Wyatt Earp* sailed from Montevideo to Magallanes, where she had been almost twelve months previously collecting the spare connecting rods for *Polar Star*! With a new captain, Captain Hartveg Olsen, *Wyatt Earp*, refuelled and with stores for two years, left port on 28 October, arriving five days later at Deception Island. Despite ice around the island and in the harbour they made it to Whalers Bay on 4 November. Here *Polar Star* was assembled and lashed to the deck.

Wyatt Earp sailed from Deception to Dundee Island, off the north-east tip of the Antarctic Peninsula, on 11 November. They based themselves at the north-west end of Dundee Island, on a sheltered passage between that island and Joinville Island. They found an ideal site for takeoff—a gently sloping, snow-covered area more or less triangular in shape which offered a runway 1,200 feet long in each of three directions.[13] On 12 November *Polar Star* was put over the side on to the sea ice and dragged half a mile to the shore. By 18 November, *Polar Star* was prepared, tested and ready for the third attempt to cross Antarctica. With good weather continuing, exploratory flights took place on 20 November (3 hours and 11 minutes) and 21 November (10 hours and 27 minutes) around the Peninsula. With hopes high, 22 November was spent servicing and checking *Polar Star.*

At 4.20 a.m. local time, on 23 November 1935, the flight took off from Dundee Island, with Lincoln Ellsworth and Herbert Hollick-Kenyon as pilots. Kenneth J. Bertrand has provided a detailed account of the flight in 'Ellsworth's Transantarctic Flight'.[14] The following paragraphs have been drawn from Bertrand's narrative.

On takeoff *Polar Star* headed south-west over the Prince Gustav Channel. Across the Weddell Sea they maintained an altitude of 7,500 feet and an indicated air speed of 126 mph. They crossed the Larsen Ice Shelf, went higher and were able to see glacier-filled valleys. They crossed George VI Sound and the English Coast and lost use of the radio (later determined to be a defective switch on the antenna lead). After 13 hours they decided to land as visibility was poor. They made camp and stayed for 19 hours. They took off before noon on 24 November but poor weather forced a landing after 30 minutes.

They stayed here for three days and late on 27 November took off again and this time flew 50 minutes, landing with just enough time to tie the plane down and pitch their tent before a blizzard hit them. Another three days and a storm, which nearly buried *Polar Star*, passed. Days were spent clearing the plane of snow. The engine was started on 3 December before another storm and it was 11.38 am on 4 December, before they took off towards the Bay of Whales. Four hours later they landed to check their position and fuel and stay the night. On 5 December, at 8.58 am, they resumed the flight, now only 150 miles from the Bay of Whales. A little over an hour later their fuel ran out and they glided to a landing at 10.03 am. They spent the rest of the day securing the plane and setting up camp.

They were about 16 miles from 'Little America' but did not reach it until 15 December, after several false starts and returns to the plane. On 16 December Ellsworth (with a foot badly infected from frostbite) and Hollick-Kenyon settled in to a relatively comfortable base to await *Wyatt Earp*, which they expected to arrive in the Bay of Whales, as planned, about a month later.

When *Polar Star* lost radio contact with *Wyatt Earp*, on 23 November, only eight hours after takeoff, two plans were put into action. George Deacon, then a scientist on the R.R.S. *Discovery II*, tells what happened in his 'Report to the Royal Geographic Society' at a meeting of the Society on 9 January 1939:

> In spite of careful preparations, Ellsworth's flight was ambitious, and when his wireless messages ceased after eight hours' flying from the Weddell Sea towards the Ross Sea, there were grave fears for his safety. Sir Hubert Wilkins came northwards with Ellsworth's ship, the Wyatt Earp, to get another aeroplane from the United States, and the world's press rang with the news of a search for the missing fliers. It was then that the Australian Government approached the Governments of Great Britain and New Zealand with a view to assisting in the search, and the action taken was so swift that we were sailing from Melbourne with two aeroplanes, seven airmen, and three months' stores less than three weeks after we had received the first telegram at the ice-edge in 98°E.[15]

As *Discovery* raced to Melbourne to load extra stores, a small plane and other items needed for her dash to the Bay of Whales, Wilkins had already put his plan into action. Three days after constant efforts failed to contact *Polar Star* he ordered *Wyatt Earp* to Deception Island and then to Magallanes.

Mrs Ellsworth, in contact with Wilkins by radio, was also organising a relief party. A plane was chartered to fly them to Magallanes but crashed in the United States before it could leave. The Texaco Company offered another Northrop plane. It flew to Chile and was loaded on *Wyatt Earp*, which sailed on 22 December for Charcot Island, in the Bellingshausen Sea, en route to the Ross Sea and the Bay of Whales. Supplies had previously been left there in case *Polar Star* had problems. Pack ice again impeded progress and weather made it impossible for the plane to be used. After waiting several days, Wilkins put *Wyatt Earp* on a course directly to the Bay of Whales. She arrived on 19 January 1936, three days before she was expected under Ellsworth's original plan!

Discovery reached the Bay of Whales at 9.30 pm on 15 January, several days before *Wyatt Earp*. George Deacon (later Sir George), in charge of the scientists on the *Discovery*, describes the scene:

> Soon we were able to make out a tent on the top of the ice-cliffs … To make sure that the two fliers, Ellsworth and his pilot, Hollick-Kenyon, were safe, Douglas and Murdoch flew over Admiral Byrd's old base camp at Little America, some 5 or 6 miles away. Soon after, Hollick-Kenyon came off, very fit and well, and we learned that Ellsworth was well except for an injured foot.[16]

> Ellsworth was brought aboard Discovery the following day and, later that day, 17 January, the ship left the Bay for scientific work in the region north of the barrier.[17] Discovery returned to the Bay on 20 January, in company with Wyatt Earp now arrived on the scene. From on board Discovery, F. D. Ommanney describes the Wyatt Earp:

> The little ship now forging southward through the ice after us bore the illustrious name of this legendary figure. We met her after a short scientific cruise in the Ross Sea. It was a cold, grey, foggy day and we could see through glasses, when she was still a long way off,

the words 'Ellsworth Expedition' blazoned in huge white letters on her black sides. She was a sealer and had a stout wooden hull, a fine, sturdy little ship. Her diesel engine shot upwards little sharp puffs of smoke from her funnel and amidships she carried the Texaco 20, a Northrop monoplane, which also wore its name in huge letters on its fuselage.[18]

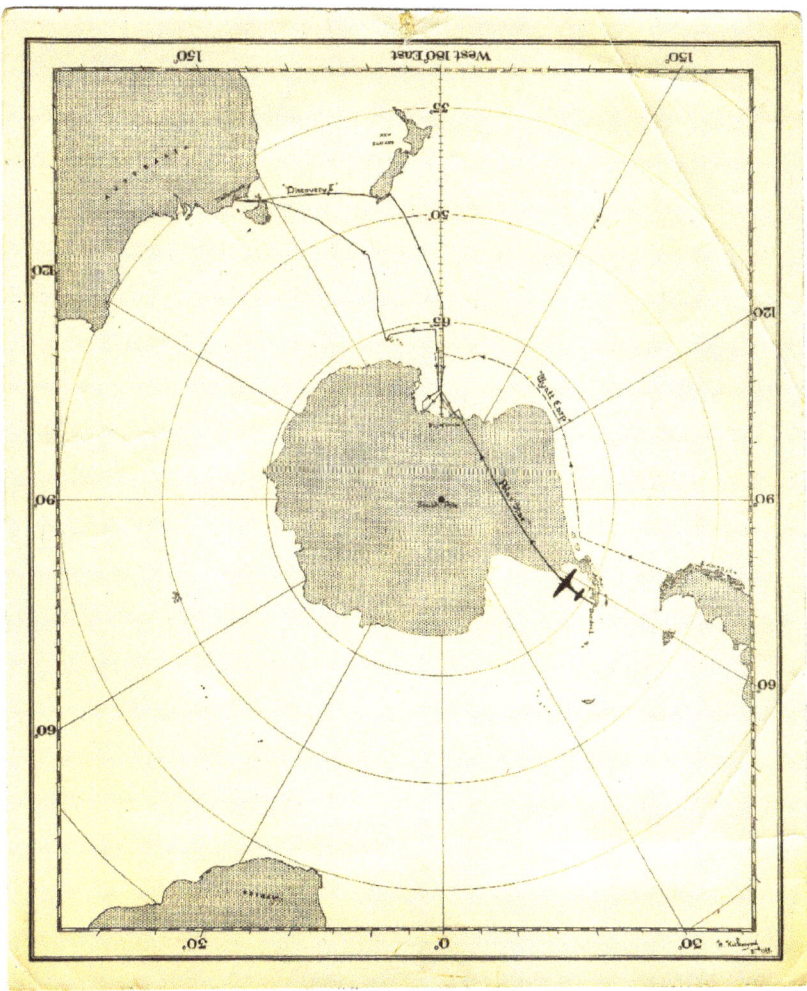

The back of the photo has a hand-written note: *Tracks of Ellsworth's Trans Antarctic Flight and of relief vessels 'Wyatt Earp' and R.R.S. 'Discovery II' in 1935–36*. (Author's personal papers, from *Discovery II*.)

On the night of 21 January, Discovery gave a farewell dinner to those on the *Wyatt Earp* and sailed very early next day (12.40 am). Lincoln Ellsworth decided to return to Australia on *Discovery*. Some scientific work, landings and surveys, in the Balleny Islands, were conducted en route. They arrived in Melbourne on 16 February 1936. All the Melbourne and many other Australian and overseas newspapers carried stories of the successful mission with headlines such as 'Epic Battle in Icy Wastes', 'Month in Hut Under the Snow', and 'Thousands Greet Ship'. The *Herald* (Melbourne) had stories on several pages as well as a full-page spread of photographs:

> The Royal Research ship Discovery II, flying the American flag from her track and the flag of the Falkland Islands from her stern, berthed at Nelson Pier, Williamstown, at 10 a.m. today, bringing with her Lincoln Ellsworth, the American aviator-explorer of the Antarctic and members of the R.A.A.F. detachment who rescued him from Little America.[19]

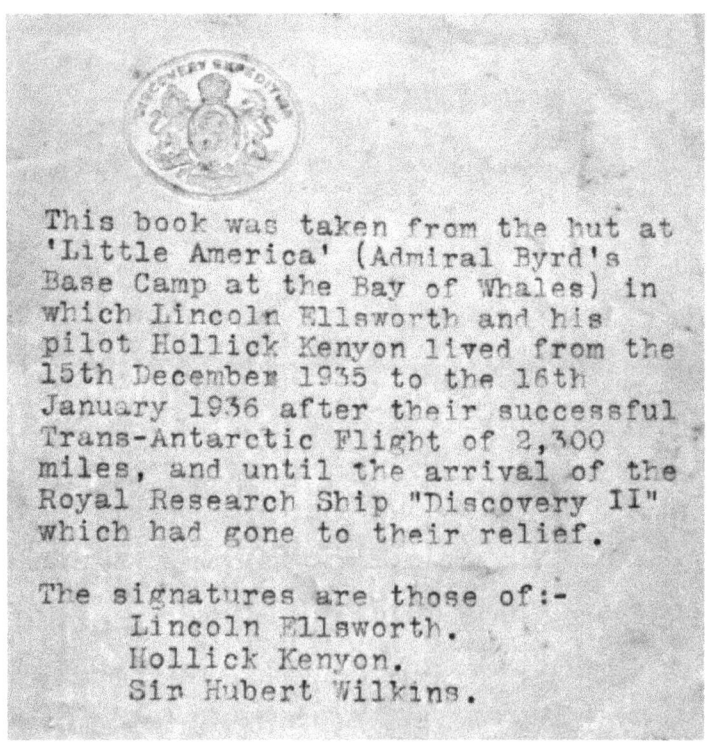

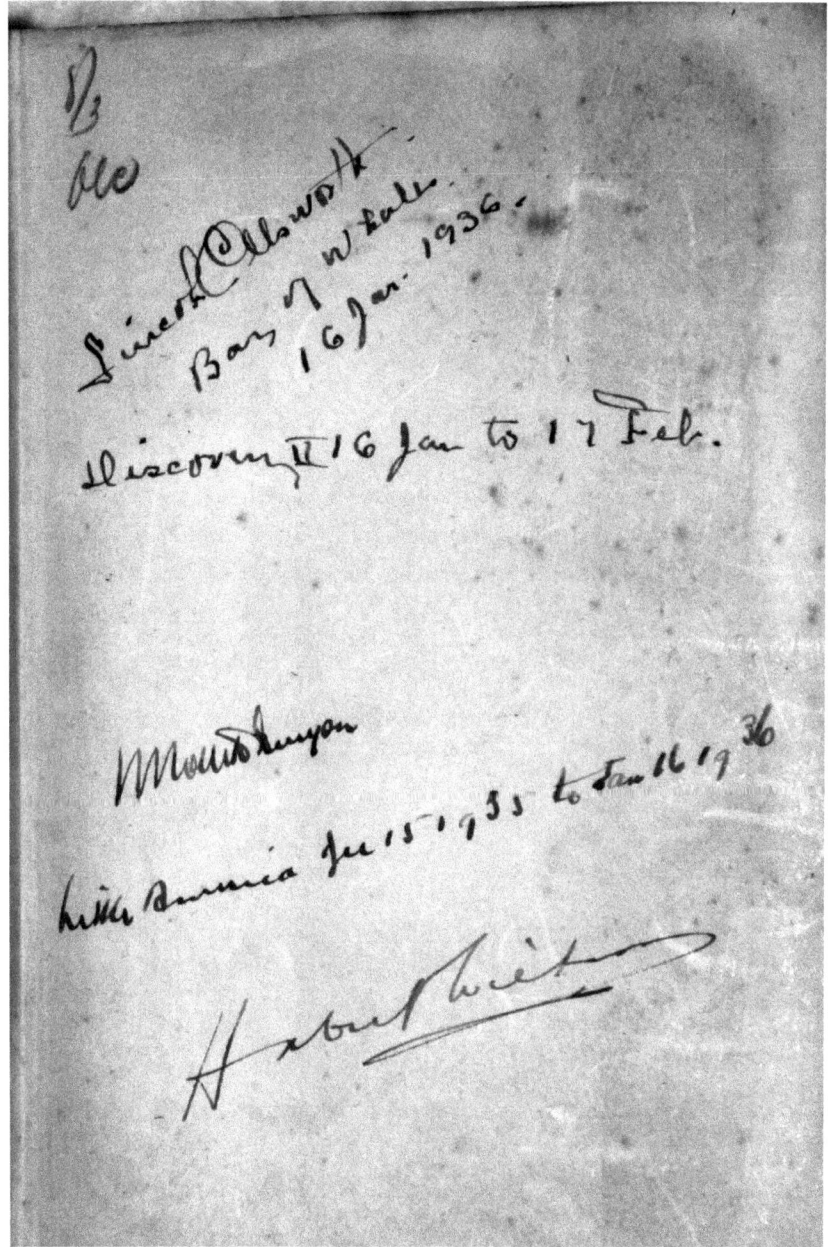

This image and the previous one relate to the book, *The Flying Inn* by G. K. Chesterton, which was taken from 'Little America' by a member of the crew of *Discovery II*. Details are recorded on an inserted sheet of 'Discovery Expedition' letterhead (see image on p. 36 opp.). The fly leaf is signed by Lincoln Ellsworth, Herbert Hollick-Kenyon and Sir Hubert Wilkins. (Author's personal papers.)

And on another page of the same paper:

> Australia's welcome to Lincoln Ellsworth was extended officially by the Minister for Defence (Mr Parkhill), representatives of the State Government, the Services, the University, learned societies and leaders of former Commonwealth expeditions to Antarctica.
>
> Thousands of people, including the pupils of local schools, surged round the barricades placed on the ramps and … leading to Nelson Pier, and the impatience with the police control that barred them from the official enclosure, from which the addresses of welcome were broadcast, broke down when the explorer came into view on the bridge of the Discovery.
>
> When Discovery tied up, crowds boarded her, despite the rule of the service which debars visitors unless by special invitation, and the crew were embarrassed in their shore tasks.[20]

Sir Douglas Mawson travelled from Adelaide to welcome Ellsworth. Captain John King Davis looked after him during his stay in Melbourne. Davis had been Captain of Mawson's 1911–14 expedition ship, *Aurora*, and his 1929–30 BANZARE voyage in *Discovery I*.

On 20 February Ellsworth flew to Canberra where he was welcomed by the Prime Minister, Joseph Lyons, and the Minister for External Affairs, Senator Sir George Pearce, at a luncheon given by the Commonwealth Government at Parliament House. This probably turned out to be a useful occasion for Ellsworth, as Lyons was still Prime Minister in February 1939 when Ellsworth was intent on selling *Wyatt Earp* to the Australian Government!

Back in the Ross Sea, Hollick-Kenyon joined *Wyatt Earp* with the hope that *Polar Star* could be salvaged. Ellsworth's men managed to get one of Byrd's abandoned tractors going and took a load of fuel to the plane. It was flown to the Bay of Whales and loaded on to *Wyatt Earp*. The ship left on 30 January, via Valparaiso and the Panama Canal, and arrived in New York on 19 April. Ellsworth, having sailed from Australia on SS *Mariposa*, was there to greet his men having at last achieved his ambition of flying across the Antarctic continent. *Wyatt Earp* stayed in New York until 17 June when she sailed for England, arriving at Barrow-in-Furness, on 8 July.

Lincoln Ellsworth's Fourth Antarctic Expedition, 1938–39

A different approach

This final expedition was different to its predecessors. War was imminent and Ellsworth did not have a real goal, although he still wanted to fly across the continent via the South Pole. Instead, persuaded by Wilkins, he decided to focus his attention on American interests in the Indian Ocean sector of the Antarctic. Having spent some time in the Arctic searching for missing Russian fliers, Wilkins's reputation and his appeal to newspaper readers had revived. Ellsworth was unhappy with this. However, as in his three previous expeditions, he asked Wilkins to organise the journey and he financed it—the last Antarctic expedition of any country to be funded entirely by private money. First in Norway, then in Cape Town, Wilkins did just that, organised it, while Ellsworth spent five weeks on safari in Kenya!

The official plan for this voyage was:

> To launch a number of triangular flights into the Indian Ocean sector of Antarctica, an area of 750,000 square miles, the interior of which was then practically unknown. Of secondary importance, only because it was less certain of achievement, was Ellsworth's plan for a second transcontinental flight. If ice conditions allowed them an early start and if weather permitted, he hoped to fly from the Indian Ocean sector over the South Pole to the Bay of Whales, a distance of approximately 2,000 miles. Here he and his pilot would wait until the Wyatt Earp picked them up later in the season.[21]

Wyatt Earp had been berthed at Ålesund in Norway, her home port, following Ellsworth's third expedition. In May 1938 Wilkins visited the ship to arrange necessary maintenance for the forthcoming voyage and to obtain a new crew. Once again all were Norwegian, whaling men with Antarctic experience. The Captain, Londer Johansen, had been a gunner and captain of a whale catcher in the Antarctic. Several of the crew had been on previous Ellsworth expeditions. J. H. Lymburner, reserve pilot on the previous voyage joined as chief pilot, and Sir Hubert Wilkins was again technical adviser and manager. Lincoln Ellsworth was organiser, leader and aerial navigator.

After refit, *Wyatt Earp* returned to New York from Norway, to the Floyd Bennett Field seaplane base in Brooklyn on 12 August 1938. She loaded stores as well as two aircraft, a Northrop 'Delta 1D' and a smaller Aeronca Model K, a two-seater scouting plane. Both planes had wheels, pontoons and skis and two-way radios giving them alternative take-off and landing options and better communications. *Wyatt Earp* sailed on 16 August for Cape Town, via Pernambuco, Brazil. Ellsworth joined the ship in Cape Town, from his hunting trip in Kenya, and Sir Hubert Wilkins flew in from Australia.

At this time the United States State Department decided they should start claiming land in the Antarctic. Unknown to Wilkins, the American Consul in Cape Town asked Ellsworth to claim any unexplored land for the United States, whether or not it lay in territory already claimed by another country! Ellsworth, in a meeting, was told that the government role must remain secret and that it would not admit to being involved should it become known. 'Ellsworth was not even given a copy of the instructions for fear they may become known to a foreigner. It is clear they meant Wilkins, for the land in question had already been claimed by Australia.'[22] Ellsworth was apparently enthusiastic despite knowing Wilkins regarded their proposed destination as Australian claimed territory. In fact, Wilkins states:

> Before leaving New York he had published a statement (which I had helped to prepare) in which it was said that he would not while on this expedition claim any land. He left New York with a definite understanding with me that he would make only one flight of not more than 500 miles inland from the coast of the Antarctic, starting from some point near Enderby Land and would leave the coast on the return journey not later than January 15th, 1939.[23]

The fourth Ellsworth Expedition sailed from Cape Town at noon on 29 October 1938, for the Kerguelen Islands. Just over two weeks later, after worse than normal rough weather encountered in the 'Roaring Forties', *Wyatt Earp* moored in Royal Sound. Three days were spent here while work was carried out on the engine and the freshwater tanks were filled. Fuel oil that had been carried on deck was transferred to the bunkers in the expectation of even heavier seas and storms. Plenty of rabbits, teal and even some Ross seals were added to the food supplies. Despite the relatively sheltered harbour, several gales hit them with snow and winds of more than 60 mph. Both anchors and three heavy mooring lines, both bow and stern, were required.

On 17 November *Wyatt Earp* left the Kerguelen Islands for Heard Island but three days of even more bad weather made landing impossible. On 20 November *Wyatt Earp* reached the edge of the pack ice, meeting it much further north than expected. It took forty-five days to pass through this 800 mile wide barrier, sometimes drifting with the pack, sometimes making no progress at all. During one drifting phase, two hardwood planks were found missing from the outer sheathing on the bow, ripped off by the ice. The Norwegian crew knew what to do and how to do it, even on a 400 ton ship at sea in the Antarctic:

> With a sling about a heavy mass of ice and a block and tackle to the mast head, the ship was careened, and by shifting oil and supplies from one side of the ship to the other we brought the damaged part above the water line and undertook repairs.
>
> Standing on a convenient ice floe the carpenter chiseled out the damaged parts and fitted in new planks and now the ship is as sound as she was when we entered the ice.[24]

Finally, on 1 January 1939, they reached the Antarctic coast—well, almost. The Aeronca made a flight and, on 3 January, they were able to moor the ship against the ice in Prydz Bay. There was plenty of ice that looked good for the plane to use for takeoff, but it was only one year old and Ellsworth worried it would not take the weight of the Northrop Delta plane. The plane was brought on deck and assembly began, however. While moored here Ellsworth went ashore on one of the Svenner Islands to collect geological specimens.

Wyatt Earp moved to the Rauer Islands and on 5 January, was moored to level ice which, with nearby islands, made a protected harbour. About

200 yards from the ship was a huge, grounded iceberg, broken off from a nearby glacier tongue. Ellsworth decided to try the ice for takeoff, calling it 'the only possible flying field in this vicinity'. The big plane assembled on deck was now made ready for flight but as they prepared to put her on to the ice, the weather turned against them. Both planes were secured and, again, Ellsworth and others visited some of the Rauer Islands to collect geological specimens.

On 7 January the weather was still not good enough for flying. Early that morning they became alarmed when the big iceberg, presumed grounded, began to move, endangering the ship. *Wyatt Earp* moved urgently astern, away from possible disaster.

Ellsworth could no longer keep his secret. He told Wilkins he intended to set foot on and claim the land Mawson had only seen from the coast. Wilkins was in a difficult position. While as a paid adviser to Ellsworth, he also had loyalty to his own country. And he, too, had a secret! He had instructions from the Australian Government. In Wilkins's 'Report of the Ellsworth Antarctic Flight Expedition, 1938–39' to the Australian Government he wrote:

> January 8th. With Pilot J. H. Lymburner as a witness I landed on the northernmost island of the group marked as Rauer on Lars Christensen's chart.
>
> ... I flew the flag of the Commonwealth of Australia and then deposited the flag and a record of the visit in a small aluminium container.
>
> The container is placed at the foot of a rock about three feet high and covered with small stones. A small cairn of stones was erected about 25 yards to the southward of the deposit.[25]

Still waiting for suitable flying conditions they had to move again on 9 January as a large and heavy ice floe was forced upon them by several icebergs. The new mooring had no suitable flying area, weather conditions were poor anyway and more waiting ensued. Wilkins and Lymburner, nevertheless, made another similar landing and deposited a record of their visit at the west end of the Vestfold Mountains. With a wind change *Wyatt Earp* returned to the first mooring to discover the fast ice had broken loose and the bay ice, from which they planned to fly, had broken up. With the scouting plane on 10 January they sighted a suitable area and, using a small motor boat, were able to lead *Wyatt Earp* to a mooring against flat ice. On 11 January they finally found an ice edge suitable to land the Northrop airplane and it was unloaded, test flown and departed on an inland flight at 6 p.m. Wilkins again took the opportunity to make a claim for Australia.

> Meanwhile I proceeded to near the eastern end of the snow-free land at the edge of the continental ice-cap—presumably the mainland—and at the top of a dyke which appears black against the surrounding granite and which extends vertically from sea level—where it is four inches wide—to the top of the hill where it is about four feet wide, I flew a large Commonwealth of Australia flag and then deposited it together with a record.[26]

He recorded that he had 'put foot on the Antarctic mainland in several places and upon several islands' and, 'having flown the flag of Australia, leave it with this record'. A handwritten note in the margin of the file copy of Wilkins's Report states: 'This is the cairn discovered by the Davis party on 8/5/1957'. Under the heading, 'Explorers Find Wilkins' Flag in Antarctica', the *Canberra Times* of 21 May 1957, recorded the finding.

Ellsworth decided to search for a site where a ski takeoff might be possible. *Wyatt Earp* headed northwest from the Rauer Islands along the coast of the Vestfold Hills. Lymburner in the Aeronca was able to takeoff from the sea for a flight of one hour and 40 minutes. He found a small fjord which he thought might be used as a takeoff site.

Wyatt Earp made a difficult, five-hour trip through ever changing ice conditions. During the night of 10 January they kept the ship moored against the ice as strong winds and heavy seas caused the ice edges to crumble. When another iceberg threatened them they moved cautiously into a small sheltered bight where the ice met up with solid rock. The ice which they had found gave an indication it might be suitable for a ski takeoff. It was short and would not allow a full load of fuel but, on 11 January, about noon, the Northrop was lowered to the ice ready for a test run—having not been flown since New York! The return of the test flight confirmed the poor condition of the ice and that the weather was clouding up in the north. It appeared clear to the south so Ellsworth and Lymburner took off with fuel for three hours and stores for two men for five weeks. Details of this flight can be found in 'Ellsworth's Last Antarctic Expedition'.[27]

After half the fuel supply was used Ellsworth estimated they were 210 miles from the coast. At this point they had to turn back And, at this point, Ellsworth made formal claim to the territory which he had just discovered. He dropped a brass cylinder containing the following words:

> To whom it may concern: Having flown on a direct course from latitude 68:30 south, longitude 79:00 east, to latitude 72 degrees south, longitude 79 east, I drop this record, together with the flag of the United States of America, and claim for my country, so far as this act allows, the area south of latitude 70 to a distance of 150 miles east and 150 miles west of my line of flight and to a distance of 150 miles south of latitude 72 south, longitude 79 east which I claim to have explored, dated Jan. 11, 1939. Lincoln Ellsworth.[28]

Lymburner and Ellsworth flew back over their outward course and arrived directly over the ship. They circled a few times before landing. High winds were causing *Wyatt* Earp to bash against the ice, from which pieces were breaking off. It was clear this flying field would not be used again. The plane was loaded and the moorings cast off.

> On 12 January Wilkins radioed a confidential message to government officials in Canberra, urging Australia to establish a winter base in order to challenge Ellsworth's claims. He sought £15,000 to purchase all Ellsworth's equipment and offered, without consulting Suzannne, to set up the base himself. The government found the idea of bases too expensive, but at Wilkins' suggestion agreed to make an offer to purchase the Wyatt Earp to raise the Australian flag over Antarctica in a more permanent sense.[29]

The storm lasted for two days and then the First Mate Liavaag had an accident, when he and two others were chipping ice pieces from a small iceberg to put in the freshwater tank. He was caught between two pieces of ice and his knee was crushed. He needed surgery of a kind not available on *Wyatt Earp*.[30] Ellsworth gave up further hopes of flying and directed the ship to head for the nearest hospital—in Hobart. The return voyage started well but overnight on 14 January *Wyatt Earp* met very heavy seas, which stove in the bridge and did other damage. On the afternoon of 15 January they encountered heavy pack ice. But, after five days through the heavy pack with snow squalls and poor visibility they were in open sea and, on 4 February 1939, *Wyatt Earp* docked in Hobart.

Ellsworth publicly reasserted his territorial claim and increased the area involved from 80,000 square miles to 430,000 square miles. This was immediately disputed by the Australian Government and, even before *Wyatt Earp* had reached Hobart, Sir Douglas Mawson was urging the Australian Government to buy the ship for Antarctic exploration.

Following the sale of *Wyatt Earp* to the Australian Government (see next chapter) the 'Ellsworth Expedition' was disbanded. Ellsworth later announced plans for another expedition but, with the outbreak of war, these plans were later cancelled. Lincoln Ellsworth arrived in Los Angeles on 20 March 1939. On 18 April 1939 Ellsworth gave a full report of the four expeditions to the Department of State, dated 17 April 1939. His plane, *Polar Star*, is in the Smithsonian National Air and Space Museum. Lincoln Ellsworth died in New York on 26 May 1951.

Endnotes

1. Jeff Maynard, *Antarctica's Lost Aviator*, Pegasus Books, 2019, p. 87.
2. antarctic-circle.org/ships.htm.
3. *Daily News* (Perth), 18 December 1933, p. 7.
4. https//www.south-pole.com/p0000110.htm.
5. https://www.south-pole.com/p0000110.htm.
6. https//www.south-pole.com/p0000110.htm.
7. Simon Nasht, *The Last Explorer*, pp.181–184.
8. In the back right hand corner you can see the edge of the hanger where BAS (British Antarctic Survey) kept their single engine Otter aircraft. Just beyond that is the old 'airstrip' which Sir Hubert Wilkins used in December 1928. Personal email from Greg Mortimer.
9. https//www.south-pole.com/p0000110.htm.

10   The town of Punta Arenas was renamed Magallanes in 1927 but returned to its previous name in 1938.
11   Kenneth J. Bertrand, *Americans in Antarctica 1775–1948*, American Geographical Society Special Publication No.39, 1971, p. 366.
12   Lincoln Ellsworth, *Beyond Horizons*, Doubleday, Doran & Company, Inc., 1938, p. 291.
13   Kenneth J. Bertrand, 'Ellsworth's Transantarctic Flight' in *Americans in Antarctica 1775–1948*, p. 373.
14   Kenneth J. Bertrand, 'Ellsworth's Transantarctic Flight' in *Americans in Antarctica 1775–1948*.
15   There were two ships named *Discovery* both involved in Australian Antarctic voyages. *Discovery I* was Mawson's ship on both his BANZARE voyages (1929–31). With *Discovery II* on this rescue mission it is sometimes confusing. In this chapter *Discovery II* is referred to as *Discovery*.
16   G.E.R. Deacon, 'The Antarctic Voyages of R.R.S. *Discovery II* and R.R.S. *William Scoresby*, 1935–37' in *The Geographical Journal*, Vol.93, No.3 (March, 1939), p. 190.
17   The 'barrier' is the Ross Ice Shelf, the largest area of floating ice in the Antarctic. Originally called 'The Barrier' as it barred ships sailing further south.
18   F.D. Ommanney, *South Latitude*, Longmans Green & Co, London, 1938, p. 211.
19   *Herald* (Melbourne), 17 February 1936, p. 1.
20   *Herald* (Melbourne), 17 February 1936, p. 2.
21   Kenneth J. Bertrand, 'The Ellsworth Antarctic Expedition, 1938–1939' in *Americans in Antarctica, 1755–1948*, p. 395.
22   Simon Nasht, *The Last Explorer Hubert Wilkins Australia's Unknown Hero*, Hodder Australia, 2005, p. 271.
23   Wilkins, 'Report of the Ellsworth Antarctic Flight Expedition, 1938–39' to the Australian Minister for External Affairs dated 6 February 1939, National Archives of Australia A 1838,1495/1 ANNEX D, p. 2.
24   Kenneth J. Bertrand, 'Ellsworth's Transantarctic Flight' in *Americans in Antarctica 1775–1948*, p. 400, from *New York Times*, 3 January 1939, p. 5.
25   Australian Archives, A1838, 1495/1 ANNEX D. p. 6.
26   Australian Archives, A1838, 1495/1 ANNEX D. p. 9.
27   Kenneth J. Bertrand, 'Ellsworth's Transantarctic Flight' in *Americans in Antarctica 1775–1948*, pp.402–403.
28   *New York Times*, 13 January 1939, p. 21.
29   Simon Nasht, *The Last Explorer*, Hodder Australia, 2005, p. 272.
30   When they reached Hobart Dr J. H. Gaha, MLC, the Tasmanian Minister for Health, operated on First Mate Liavaag assisted by *Wyatt Earp*'s doctor, Dr Harmon Rhoads Jr. Despite the three week delay between accident and operation, and the severity of the injury, the operation was successful. *Mercury* (Hobart), 7 February 1939, p. 9.

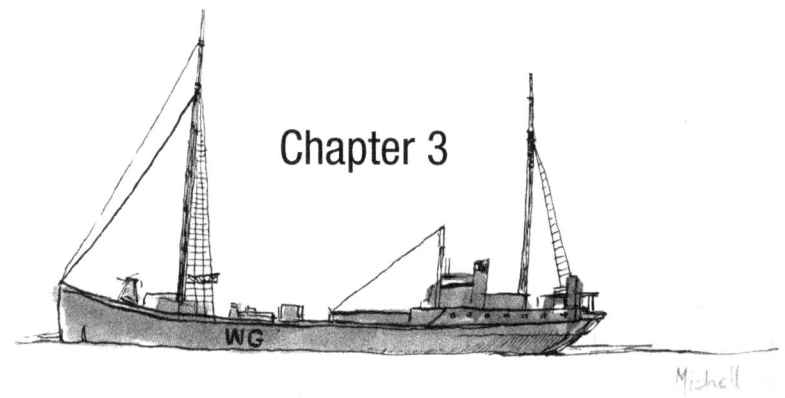

Chapter 3

War service and Sea Scouts

RAFA *Wongala*

HMAS *Wongala*

SSTS *Wongala*

HMAS *Wongala*

HMAS *Wyatt Earp*

Following his third Antarctic Expedition, in February 1936, and from which the 'lost fliers' were rescued by *Discovery II* from the Bay of Whales, Lincoln Ellsworth returned to a hero's welcome in Melbourne. Later he flew to Canberra for lunch at Parliament House, hosted by Prime Minister Joseph Lyons and the Australian Government. Others at this lunch included Mr Richard Casey (later Lord Casey), Treasurer of Australia, and Lieutenant Hill, RN, Captain of *Discovery II*, who was appointed an Officer of the Order of the British Empire (OBE) for his role in the rescue of the stranded fliers.

Three years later, and well before the end of the fourth Lincoln Ellsworth Antarctic Expedition, *Wyatt Earp*, which arrived in Hobart on 4 February 1939, was being brought to the attention of the Australian Government and the Australian public. Throughout January Australian newspapers, as diverse as the *Recorder* in Port Pirie and the *Kalgoorlie Miner*, were printing stories of 'Sir Douglas Mawson's Plea' that the Australian Government should purchase *Wyatt Earp* on her return from the Antarctic. On 19 January, under 'Constant Contact With Antarctic', it was reported that Sir Douglas had asked the Commonwealth Treasurer, Mr R. G. Casey to buy the ship as part of a wider plan for annual scientific trips to the South and to build meteorological stations on the Antarctic continent as well as at Macquarie Island and Heard Island. It was also reported that 'Mr Ellsworth would sell to the Commonwealth the ship at less than £4000, a fraction of her real value'.[1] Sir Hubert Wilkins kept in contact with people in Australia by radiograms during the voyage and submitted a report to the Australian Government upon his return.[2]

The *Chronicle* (Adelaide), on 2 February 1939, under the heading 'Quick Decision Needed' said that *Wyatt Earp* 'is expected to reach Hobart within a fortnight'. The ship was returning as fast as possible with an injured crew member in need of urgent medical treatment. The article continued that Sir Douglas Mawson had earlier suggested the Commonwealth Government should purchase *Wyatt Earp* for use in the Antarctic and survey work on the Australian coast. He suggested that a quick decision was needed because Lincoln Ellsworth would put the ship up for sale in the United States if Australia did not want it.

Ellsworth must have already been thinking of his next trip and his next ship as, a few months later, the *Sydney Morning Herald* reported from New York under the heading, 'Wintering at South Pole. Ellsworth's Plans. "Like to Dig in Polar Ice-Cap"':

> Before leaving for Norway to secure a base ship to replace the *Wyatt Earp* (which was purchased by the Commonwealth Government), Mr. Lincoln Ellsworth announced plans to spend the winter of 1940–41 at the South Pole. ... The fifth Ellsworth expedition will be independent of the U.S. Government expedition, under Rear-Admiral Byrd (which will leave in October) but it will co-operate with it closely.[3]

When *Wyatt Earp* reached Hobart, Ellsworth lost no time in publicly reasserting his claim, on behalf of the United States of America, of the land over which he had flown on 11 January. And he increased the area involved, to cover all that he could see as well as that he had flown over, from his original claim of 80,000 square miles to 430,000 square miles! The Australian Government immediately rejected the claim and Sir Douglas Mawson had another reason to urge the government to buy a ship capable of visiting the Antarctic continent. Australia needed a permanent presence there.

From early in February 1939, Australian newspapers ran frequent short articles over the next few weeks concerning *Wyatt Earp*. 'Wyatt Earp Before Cabinet' (*Daily Telegraph*, Sydney, 6 February), 'Cabinet and The Wyatt Earp' (*News*, Adelaide, 6 February), 'Purchase of Wyatt Earp Sir Douglas Mawson Delighted' (*Advertiser*, Adelaide, 9 February), 'The Wyatt Earp—Exploration Value' (*The Age*, Melbourne, 9 February). And in *The Mercury*, also on 9 February, 'Wyatt Earp—Departure for Sydney' with the information that 'In the half darkness of last evening the Wyatt Earp, Lincoln Ellsworth's exploration ship which has been purchased by the Commonwealth Government, left Queen's Pier, Hobart, for Sydney.' Again, the *Kalgoorlie Miner* seemed to be quick with the news:

> 'Mr. Lincoln Ellsworth has made a generous gesture to assist Australian scientific investigation, and I am delighted that the Commonwealth Government has taken the opportunity of purchasing so valuable and fully equipped a vessel as the Wyatt Earp,' said the professor of geology and mineralogy at the University of Adelaide, Sir Douglas Mawson yesterday.
>
> The purchase price from Mr. Lincoln Ellsworth is about £4400. 'I am convinced that it was a first-class purchase,' said Sir Douglas Mawson. 'I believe that it has been sold on the understanding that the vessel will be used for scientific investigation.
>
> The aircraft bought with the vessel, a Northrop all metal low wing, and a small Aeronca scouting machine, are of recent design and, when new, were valued at £17,000.'[4]

The report continues, quoting Sir Douglas Mawson:

> 'Previously, the obtaining of a suitable vessel and brining [sic] it to Australia has been a most expensive item and crippled previous explorations before they left for the Antarctic. However, the future proposals for the use of the Wyatt Earp eliminate the biggest expenditure.

> The Wyatt Earp is an inexpensive vessel to run and the monthly cost would be not more than half of that of vessels used previously on Australian Antarctic expeditions. The reasons are that the ship is driven by Diesel engines, requiring a small staff to handle fuel. The sails are rigged fore and aft with no spars, and are handled from the deck, obviating the employment of high skilled seamen.'

Various newspaper reports noted the arrival of *Wyatt Earp* in Sydney on 12 February. The *Courier-Mail* (Brisbane) reported on 3 March that Sir Douglas Mawson had spent the two previous days in discussions with 'Mr. Lincoln Ellsworth and Sir Hubert Wilkins and made a thorough inspection of the *Wyatt Earp* and the two aeroplanes which were included in the equipment purchased by the Commonwealth Government from Mr. Ellsworth'. Sir Douglas Mawson commented, on 6 March, that he had visited the ship in Sydney, and that no plans for Antarctic exploration would be considered until the report of the marine surveyor was received.

Under the heading, 'Wyatt Earp for the Navy', the *Singleton Argus* stated: 'Immediate use is to be found for the *Wyatt Earp* by the Defence Department. The Naval Board has applied for the ship for the work to which she is specially adapted, and the Government has agreed to hand it over.'[5] The report then quoted the Treasurer (Mr Casey), who said that such arrangement 'need not interfere with plans for using the ship for Antarctic exploration in the summer'. He added that he was 'not in a position to say what type of duties the vessel would be used for by the Navy'.

While these discussions were taking place, Sir Hubert Wilkins decided to become further involved and submitted his ideas directly to the Prime Minister. He suggested that *Wyatt Earp* should:

> undertake a two months' cruise between Sydney and Fremantle, starting about the middle of May, and experimenting en route in handline fishing at various points of interest to the fishing industry.
>
> It is then suggested that the Wyatt Earp should undertake a cruise to the edge of the Antarctic pack ice, to make meteorological observations. 'Later in the year a meteorological base might be established at Macquarie Island,' says Sir Hubert Wilkins in his letter.[6]

Chapter 3 — War service and Sea Scouts

With further suggestions from Sir Hubert, the article concluded that his 'plan will be referred to Cabinet'.

Slowly more information became available. On 9 May, the *Kalgoorlie Miner* hinted:

> The Antarctic exploration vessel, Wyatt Earp, may be used as a munitions transport. At present interstate steamship services are used to convey munitions and explosives between Australian ports at rates which are commensurate with the risks. The Wyatt Earp, which was purchased at almost a gift price by the Commonwealth Government, will make the Defence Department independent.

And so *Wyatt Earp* was transferred to the Royal Australian Navy and a lengthy debate followed about what her name should be. On Department of Defence Minute Paper, with Navy Office typed at the top, the Director of Ordnance, Torpedoes and Mines, wrote, on 4 July 1939, to Head of 'N' (Navy), Secretary, Naval Board and 1st Naval Member, under the subject 'WYATT EARP—USE AS AMMUNITION CARRIER' as follows:

Submitted

1. As this vessel is to belong to the Navy, I recommend she be given a less offensive name.
2. I suggest 'BOOMERANG', as a primitive type of Australian ammunition, also envisaging a possible recoil if the ship turns out a failure.

Head of 'N' has initialled that he has seen the Minute. One of the other two addressees has written: 'I strongly favour discarding the name Wyatt Earp, and consider BOOMERANG a good proposal.' While the Navy Department was thinking about what to do with the ship, Sir Hubert Wilkins sent a telegram to the Commonwealth Government suggesting he be given the use of 'Wyatt Earp and land, the base which he would maintain with private funds, in the Australian Antarctic territory.'[7] Part of this suggestion was that 'Wyatt Earp be made available to deliver his party at a base to be approved by the Commonwealth Government. It would be necessary for the Wyatt Earp to visit this base in each of the two succeeding seasons.'

The submission came before Cabinet on 3 August 1939, from the Department of External Affairs, signed by the Minister, H. G. Gullett [sic H.S.], (Sir Henry). It explains that:

> Wyatt Earp with two aeroplanes was purchased from Ellsworth in January of this year at a cost of £4,400. In May the vessel was transferred to the Defence Department for the transport of explosive and ammunition and general naval supplies between the various Australian ports on condition that the vessel would be made available for Antarctic exploration work for three or four months each year. It is the view of the Naval Board that if the Government desires to afford the facilities requested by Sir Hubert Wilkins the vessel should not be leased to Sir Hubert Wilkins but sold to him on the same terms as she was purchased by the Commonwealth.

While the submission notes that Sir Hubert has already 'done useful propaganda and paved some of the way for the establishment of these stations' it has the handwritten words 'Not Approved' at the end.[8]

Things moved slowly! The Meeting of the Naval Board, held at Navy Office, on Saturday 9 September 1939, (six days after the declaration of War) in Board Minute No.173, records:

> M.V. "WYATT EARP"
>
> Consideration was given to the use to which this vessel could be put and it was DECIDED as follows :-
>
> 1. The vessel to be used to convey ammunition, explosives, and government stores to and from Australia and possibly to New Zealand. It is observed that the Government has approved the vessel being so used.
> 2. The vessel to be run as a Fleet Auxiliary, flying the blue ensign of the Commonwealth, manned with a civilian crew. Consideration was given to the practicability of utilising a Naval crew, but the difficulties were too numerous.
> 3. The vessel to be refitted so as to comply with requirements of the Navigation Act.

Chapter 3 — War service and Sea Scouts

The name of the vessel to be changed to R.A.F.A. "BOOMERANG".

> It was not thought necessary to appoint Agents for the vessel, as the Department could arrange for the carry out of the necessary duties.

On 19 September, the Permanent Head (Secretary) of the Department of Defence, Mr F. G. Shedden, wrote to the Registrar of Shipping, at Customs House, Sydney, making application for the MOTOR SHIP "BOOMERANG" (late "WYATT EARP") to be registered under the Merchant Shipping Act 1894. He gives the following particulars:

(i)	Name and description of the ship	"Boomerang" (late "Wyatt Earp") Diesel driven single screw wooden vessel of 402.16 gross tonnage and 274.68 register tonnage.
(ii)	Time and place where ship was built	Built in 1918/1919 in Belsones ship yard, Norway.
(iii)	Nature of Title	Purchased by the Commonwealth of Australia from Lincoln Ellsworth of New York, United States of America.
(iv)	Documents of Title	(a) Copy Certificate of Nationality of Motor Ship "Wyatt Earp" certified by Royal Norwegian Consulate General;
		(b) Duplicate Bill of Sale dated 28th February, 1939 signed by Sir Hubert Wilkins as Manager of Wyatt Earp A/S Ltd and Lincoln Ellsworth disposing of the Motor Ship "Wyatt Earp" to Mr Lincoln Ellsworth;
		(c) Agreement dated 3rd March, 1939 between Lincoln Ellsworth of the first part Sir Hubert Wilkins of the second part and the Commonwealth of Australia of the third part assigning the Motor Ship "Wyatt Earp" to the Commonwealth of Australia.
		(iv) Name of Master—Frederick K. Baxter
		(v) The ship is controlled by the Department of Defence, and Frederick Geoffrey Shedden is the Permanent Head of the Department.

This letter seems to refute the much quoted story that Ellsworth gave *Wyatt Earp* to Sir Hubert Wilkins on their return to Australia and Wilkins immediately sold the ship to the Australian Government, for his own profit. It also puts the date of the sale to the Commonwealth of Australia as 3 March, and confirms Sir Douglas Mawson's high profile role in the matter, given his statements to the press around that time. And he did not give up on his campaign for a permanent Australian base on the Antarctic continent.

COMMONWEALTH OF AUSTRALIA.

DEPARTMENT OF DEFENCE.

The Registrar of Shipping,
   Customs House,
     SYDNEY.   N.S.W.

Dear Sir,

               RE MOTOR SHIP "BOOMERANG" (late "WYATT EARP".)

    I hereby make application for the registration under the Merchant Shipping Act 1894 of the Motor Ship "Boomerang" and in accordance with the provisions of the Order in Council dated 8th December 1924 published in the Commonwealth of Australia Gazette No.17 dated 19th February 1925 at page 246, I furnish the following particulars :-

(i) Name and description of the ship – "Boomerang" (late "Wyatt Earp"), Diesel driven single screw wooden vessel of 402.16 gross tonnage and 274.68 register tonnage.

(ii) Time and place where ship was built – Built in 1918/1919 at Bolsones ship yard, Norway.

(iii) Nature of Title – Purchased by the Commonwealth of Australia from Lincoln Ellsworth of New York, United States of America.

Documents of Title –
(a) Copy Certificate of Nationality of Motor Ship "Wyatt Earp" certified by Royal Norwegian Consulate General;

(b) Duplicate Bill of Sale dated 28th February, 1939 signed by Sir Hubert Wilkins as Manager of Wyatt Earp A/S Ltd. and Lincoln Ellsworth disposing of the Motor Ship "Wyatt Earp" to Mr. Lincoln Ellsworth;

(c) Agreement dated 3rd March, 1939 between Lincoln Ellsworth of the first part Sir Hubert Wilkins of the second part and the Commonwealth of Australia of the third part assigning the Motor Ship "Wyatt Earp" to the Commonwealth of Australia.

(iv) Name of Master – Frederick K. Baxter.

(v) The ship is controlled by the Department of Defence, and Frederick Geoffrey Shedden is the Permanent Head of that Department.

DATED this nineteenth day of September, 1939.

                   Yours truly,

Letter to Registrar of Shipping, Sydney, giving details of sale of *Wyatt Earp* by Lincoln Ellsworth to the Commonwealth of Australia. Courtesy: Naval History Section—Sea Power Centre.

It was not to be all smooth sailing, however! Over four weeks later, on 21 October, Navy Office sent a message to N.B. (Naval Board) from N.O.C.S. (Naval Officer Commanding Sydney), which was distributed to a long list of people. It reads:

> YOUR 1627/15/9 DEPUTY CROWN SOLICITOR ADVISES THAT NAME "BOOMERANG" HAS ALREADY BEEN REGISTERED FOR ANOTHER VESSEL. SUGGEST "WYATT EARP" BE RENAMED "WONGALA" WHICH IS ALSO THE ABORIGINAL NAME FOR BOOMERANG.[9]

This must have been acceptable to all concerned because on 31 October 1939, the Crown Solicitor's Office in Sydney wrote to The Secretary, Department of Defence stating that:

> further to their telephone conversation, the Registrar of Shipping had advised the *Wyatt Earp* has been registered as "Wongala" and the Certification of Registry has been delivered by hand to the Master of the Ship.

In 'Commonwealth Navy Orders' from Navy Office, Melbourne, on 21 November 1939, the following Order was promulgated:

> R.A.F.A. "WONGALA" The M.V. *Wyatt Earp* has been placed at the disposal of the Royal Australian Navy and will be run as a Fleet Auxiliary under the name of Wongala. (603/277/11.)[10]

By this date RAFA *Wongala* had already left Sydney (on 14 November), bound for Darwin with a cargo of 'stores'. It is possible that 'stores' included munitions.[11]

Wongala called at Townsville before reaching Darwin. She returned to Sydney on 11 January 1940 and must have been found unsuitable for this task as she was laid up while a further decision was made on how best to use her. Several later newspaper reports state that while in Darwin she was used for cable laying. This seems unlikely given the time frame of her return voyage. Further, there is no record of cable laying taking place in Darwin at that time, and the ship was, in any case, unsuitable for that particular task.

> NAVY OFFICE.
> DEPARTMENT OF DEFENCE.
> MINUTE PAPER.
> (This side only to be written on.)
>
> SUBJECT: "WYATT EARP" - USE AS AMMUNITION CARRIER.
>
> Head of 'N'.
> Secretary, Naval Board. *I strongly favour discarding the name Wyatt Earp, and consider BOOMERANG a good proposal.*
> 1st Naval Member.
>
> Submitted
> As this vessel is to belong to the Navy, I recommend she be given a less offensive name.
>
> 2. I suggest "BOOMERANG", as a primitive type of Australian ammunition, also envisaging a possible recoil if the ship turns out a failure.
>
> 7/7/1939.
> Director of Ordnance,
> Torpedoes and Mines.

Minute from Navy Office re 'Wyatt Earp—Use as Ammunition Carrier'—Name. Courtesy: Naval History Section—Sea Power Centre.

It may have been that a court case in which a seaman on that voyage sued the Captain for unlawful dismissal made the Navy rethink how the *Wongala* should be crewed. According to several newspaper reports early in April 1940, there had been trouble on the ship between the chief mate and a seaman, Desmond Charles Rolfe. When the ship reached Darwin Rolfe was discharged and given a passage to Sydney on another ship. He sued the Captain for 10 days' wages and compensation of an amount equivalent to a further month's wages. The reports state the ship had on board naval ratings as well as the licensed seaman who was suing, although the Naval Board Minute No.173 clearly states she was to carry a civilian crew. It may be the naval ratings were merely passengers.

During the hearing, the point was raised whether Commonwealth arbitration awards applied to vessels of His Majesty's fleet. This and other legal points will be argued further next Wednesday, to which day the hearing was adjourned.[12]

No further reports on this case have been identified in the newspapers. But there are reports of a person called Desmond Charles Rolfe appearing in several Court cases: in Nowra Court in January 1927 in breach of traffic regulations; in the District Court in Sydney in March 1928 suing the Greyhound Coursing Association to recover alleged overtime money (which he did not win); in the Commonwealth Arbitration Court in February 1941, as a member of the Seamen's Union of Australia, seeking directions regarding the conduct of the ballot for election of officers (he was a candidate for the office of general secretary); and in August 1947, in the Traffic Court, he was fined for speeding on the Harbour Bridge!

Perhaps the uncertainty of whether Commonwealth arbitration awards applied to civilians crewing ships of His Majesty's fleet was the reason behind the Naval Board decision to commission *Wongala* into the Navy and have an all Royal Australian Navy crew, even if they were mostly Naval Reserve volunteers. On 15 July 1940, HMAS *Wongala* was commissioned in Sydney as an Examination Vessel. The purpose of the Examination Service, manned by Naval Reserve volunteers, was to identify vessels wishing to enter defended ports around Australia. At the same time Port War Signal Stations were established. They had the job of identifying ships approaching ports before they were allowed to enter. If a ship could not be identified it would be directed to an examination anchorage while an investigation was carried out by an examination vessel. HMAS *Wongala* was sent to Port Adelaide, tasked with checking incoming ships, until the Examination Service was suspended at that port in 1943. From November that year until March 1944 she became a guard ship at Whyalla and patrolled the Whyalla, Port Pirie and Wallaroo areas as well as acting as 'mother ship' to the Naval Auxiliary Patrol.

While HMAS *Wongala* was armed with two guns, not all the Naval Auxiliary Patrol launches from HMAS *Torrens* defending the Adelaide port areas, had two guns, one on the bow and one on stern. Some had just one on the bow. On those vessels they would head out of port towards the sea facing any incoming vessels and at the limit of their patrol area would return to port in reverse so that the gun continued facing any 'enemy' ships. The gun could not be trained to get a clear firing line across the deck and over the stern.[13]

Wongala in dry dock, probably in Sydney before her first voyage with the Royal Australian Navy. Courtesy: Naval History Section—Sea Power Centre.

Chapter 3 War service and Sea Scouts

HMAS *Wongala*, 1940–1944. Note 12 pounder cannon/gun mounted on bow and Oerlikon machine gun on stern. Courtesy: Naval History Section—Sea Power Centre.

Little known details of the Second World War in Australia include that:

> In late 1940 two German ships "PENGVIN" and "PASSAT" entered South Australian waters and laid mine fields across Investigation Straight [sic Investigator Strait] and Backstairs Passage. As a result of this action the passenger-cargo ship "HERTFORD" was struck by a mine on December 7 and although damaged was able to be towed to Port Lincoln. Ships from HMAS TORRENS were now deployed on minesweeping duties off the South Australian Coast.
>
> In all, some forty mines were washed ashore along the South Australian coast during this period.[14]

On 26 March 1944, having finished her war duties, HMAS *Wongala* sailed to Port Adelaide, arriving the following day, and was paid off on 19 July 1944. Things continued to move slowly for this ship. It was not until six months later, on 8 February 1945, that the *Advertiser* reported that the

Chief Commissioner of the South Australian Branch of the Boy Scouts Association had announced that the Commonwealth Government had made *Wongala* available as a training ship for the Sea Scouts. On 3 March, the District Naval Officer handed the ship over to the Boy Scouts Association at Outer Harbour, where now, Sea Scout Training Ship, SSTS *Wongala* was moored. A gala occasion was reported by the *Advertiser*:

> 'This is the first time in Australia that sea scouts will have a training ship as their headquarters,' said the District Naval Officer (Cmdr S. R. Symonds) when he handed over the ship Wongala, formerly the Antarctic ship Wyatt Earp to the Boy Scouts Association at Outer Harbour on Saturday.
>
> Cmdr Symonds was greeted by a guard of honour of sea scouts, and was 'piped over the side' of the Wongala, whose decks were lined by more than 100 boys. ... The 400-ton ship was dressed with naval flags and throughout the afternoon the band of the Ex-Naval Men's Association provided music ... The white ensign of the Navy was hauled down, and the red ensign, flag of the merchant service, was flown in its stead with the Boy Scouts' flag at the stern of the ship. ... After the ceremony relatives of the scouts, officers of the Boy Scout movement and representatives of seafaring organisations were entertained at afternoon tea.[15]

Over the next two years many Sea Scout training courses were held aboard SSTS *Wongala*. During Easter 1945, 45 Sea Scouts and Sea Scout officers participated in on board instruction in seamanship as well as scout training. In total, over 400 boys trained in the ship in such topics as elementary navigation, life saving, fire drill, rigging, boatmanship and seamanship.

In February 1947, the *Advertiser* reported that 'The Wongala, which has been used for two years as a Sea Scout training ship, will be handed back to the Navy for probable use again as an exploration ship in the Antarctic.'[16] *Wongala* had at least one brush with disaster during her two years with the Sea Scouts!

> The sea scout training ship Wongala, which was blown on to a mud-bank at Outer Harbor on Friday, was floated off yesterday morning at high

tide. She is alongside at No. 4 berth Outer Harbor, and will remain there until after a ceremony on board on Sunday week.

No damage was done to the *Wongala*, although about eight feet of the keel was in the mud. In future she will have double forward moorings.[17]

It was during 1946 that Sir Douglas Mawson again stepped up his representations to the Minister for External Affairs, Dr H. V. Evatt, to support Australia's territorial claims in the Antarctic, as Norway and the United States, in particular, were taking a greater interest in the continent. On 2 December 1946 the Minister held an inter-departmental committee meeting, to which Mawson was invited.

> The committee recommended that the departments concerned should develop concrete plans for an expedition to Australian Antarctic Territory, using a naval ship equipped with a suitable aircraft. The object was to find an ice-free area on that continent that could be used as the site for a permanent base. Mawson suggested that the ship HMAS Wyatt Earp, owned by the Navy but lying uncommissioned in the Torrens River at Port Adelaide, be refitted for use by the expedition.[18]

This proposal was accepted by Cabinet on 20 December 1946 and, on 4 January 1947, the first meeting of the (Australian) Executive Committee on Exploration and Exploitation was held, chaired by the head of the Department of External Affairs, Mr W. E. Dunk. The following proposals were put forward:

- that an Executive Planning Committee be formed under the Department;
- that preliminary plans for an expedition be drawn up at an estimated cost of 250,000 pounds;
- that the ship Wyatt Earp be refitted by the Navy;
- that an LST, a Landingship, Tanks, be provided by the Navy to establish a scientific station at Macquarie Island;
- that Group Captain Stuart Campbell (RAAF retd) be seconded from his position as Director of Air Navigation and Safety in the

Department of Civil Aviation, to act as Chief Executive officer of the expedition. (Campbell had been senior aircraft pilot on Mawson's two BANZARE cruises).[19]

Things got underway quickly and in February 1947 the South Australian Boy Scouts Association received the news from the Department of the Navy that the Commonwealth Government was considering using *Wongala* for Antarctic work and needed the ship returned to the Navy so that it could be assessed for suitability and seaworthiness. The State Secretary of the Boy Scouts Association said 'that a ceremony would be held aboard at sunset on Saturday when the Scout colours and the Red Ensign would be lowered for the last time'.[20]

Back with the Royal Australian Navy as HMAS *Wongala* and found fit for Antarctic work, the Australian Government announced £150,000 for an expedition to the Antarctic in the coming summer of 1947–48:

> The Prime Minister (Mr. Chifley) announced that Cabinet had decided to allot £100,000 to the Department of External Affairs to enable early planning for the expedition.
>
> The Polar exploration ship Wyatt Earp, bought by the Commonwealth just before the war, will be used, and essential repairs estimated to cost £50,000 will be carried out by the Navy Department. . . .
>
> Cabinet decided today to reconstitute and expand a committee which has been dealing with the project. The new committee will comprise representatives of the Navy, the Air Department, the External Affairs Department, the Treasury, and the Council for Scientific and Industrial Research.
>
> Other members will be Sir Douglas Mawson, Australia's leading authority on Antarctica, who will be adviser on planning, and the people chosen to lead the expedition and the captain appointed to the Wyatt Earp.[21]

The same newspaper report outlined who else would be included in the committee, that the expeditions would be partly survey and partly scientific and that aircraft would be used extensively for survey purposes, while scientific work would concentrate on meteorology and geology.

A very extensive refit of the ship was undertaken at Port Adelaide, under the supervision of Lieutenant Commander H. F. Irwin, a Navy Engineer, who was part of the crew for the voyage to the Antarctic. Lieutenant Commander Bill Cook joined as First Lieutenant in June 1947. In an article for the Naval Historical Society of Australia, dated 31 December 1978, he gave his account of the refit and then the voyages. Writing about the work done at Port Adelaide he says:

> She was but a gutted hulk on the slipway, and the refit (a story in itself) staggered forward, beset with industrial troubles and slipping steadily behind schedule. At the conclusion of the refit there was no time for a proper shakedown, and many of our later troubles can be ascribed to this factor.
>
> It was most interesting rebuilding a ship up from the hull. None of us, except the Captain who did not join until later, had been to the Antarctic so we had to draw on our imagination and our knowledge gained from books written by those who had gone before. ... fresh water was to be a big problem, as we had no distilling plant. So we thought out a device for thawing snow and ice between the engine exhaust pipe and the outer funnel. It worked quite well, but as you know it takes masses of snow to make a gallon of water. Still we were glad of it later.
>
> Another domestic problem was that of refrigeration. One doesn't envisage using a 'fridge when thinking in terms of a voyage to Antarctica, but how do you keep meat and vegetables fresh until you reach the ice? So we made a temporary ice box out of the ship's company bathroom (a tiny structure on the upper deck) and, in Hobart, with layers of sawdust and ice, we packed the meat, butter, vegetables in perfect safety until it was cold enough to stow them on the upper deck.[22]

The Adelaide *Advertiser* reported that the ship had been stripped of her fittings and superstructure and her engines had been removed. Her two 70 foot wooden masts were about to be lifted out. Lieutenant Commander Irwin commented:

It was hoped the decks could be relaid so that work on the vessel's interior would not be delayed by winter rains.

About 50 tons of heavy anchor chain, which was used as ballast, has been lifted out, and the remaining 30 odd tons are expected to come out tomorrow ... New engines for the Wyatt Earp arrived from Sydney on Monday and are ready for installation when the vessel comes off the slips.[23]

The engine was a 450 h.p. 8 cylinder direct reversing Crossley diesel engine. The crankshaft weighed 15 tons and was not installed until 20 September. Other work included accommodation for 30 crew, a new (open) bridge and chartroom, and a scientific laboratory as well as modern equipment including an echo sounder, gyrocompass and radar. The masts, fuel and water tanks all had to be refitted. Cook recalled in his Expedition Journal:

One splendid idea we had was the galley. It was obvious that with one cook (one professional cook) on complement we should have only one galley to serve both officers and ship's company. As we expected the galley range to be alight most of the time and heat was to be a very necessary ingredient to our creature comforts, we placed the galley in the centre of the ship between the wardroom on one side and the ship's company mess on the other. We also left the bulkheads in that area unlined so the heat from the galley permeated through the steel of the bulkheads to warm the messes. It proved 100% effective and many a time after four hours on watch I stood gratefully with my back, bottom and hands against the galley bulkheads thawing out before I ate my meal.[24]

While work on the refit was in progress discussions must have been taking place on the name of the Australian ship to go to the Antarctic later in the year. On 3 June 1947, in the House of Representatives in Canberra, Mr Gil Duthie, the Labor Member for Wilmot in Tasmania, asked the Attorney General, Dr Evatt:

Why the ship associated with the projected Australian Antarctic expedition, now being fitted out at Port Adelaide, perpetuates the name of Wyatt Earp, a hard-riding, two-gun sheriff of Arizona? That was the name given to the ship by Lincoln Ellsworth. Anyway, we have plenty of gunmen in our own history.

The Attorney General and Minister for External Affairs, Dr H. V. Evatt, responded:

> I do not know the history of the person after whom the vessel *Wyatt Earp* is named, but I know that the ship was constructed some years ago, and has been selected by the committee as being suitable for the type of work on which it is to be employed. The vessel is not owned by the Australian Government, but is simply under its control. If it were a new vessel I should give consideration to the honourable member's suggestion.[25]

The Naval Board again had a decision to make on the name of the ship. More correspondence took place. In a Minute dated 9 June 1947, to DCNS (Deputy Chief of Naval Staff) and 2NM (Second Naval Member) the Director of Planning says that Group Captain Campbell has stated 'that he considers that the name is Internationally famous in Polar circles and, consequently, despite any effort on our part to re-name her she would still be known in these circles by that name, viz, 'Wyatt Earp''. Other suggested names put forward were Mawson, Flinders and Bass.

On 13 June 1947 the Naval Board wrote to Commander K. E. Oom, soon to be appointed Captain of the soon to be named HMAS *Wyatt Earp*, asking for his 'remarks on the proposal'. On 18 June he sent a signal signed as Commanding Officer of HMAS *Warrego*, which simply read: 'SUPPORTING WONGALA BACK TO WYATT EARP'.[26] In August 1947, the Secretary, Department of Navy (Mr A. R. Nankervis) wrote to the Chief Executive Officer, Group Captain Stuart Campbell, of the newly formed Australian National Antarctic Research Expedition (ANARE), based at Victoria Barracks in St Kilda Road, Melbourne:

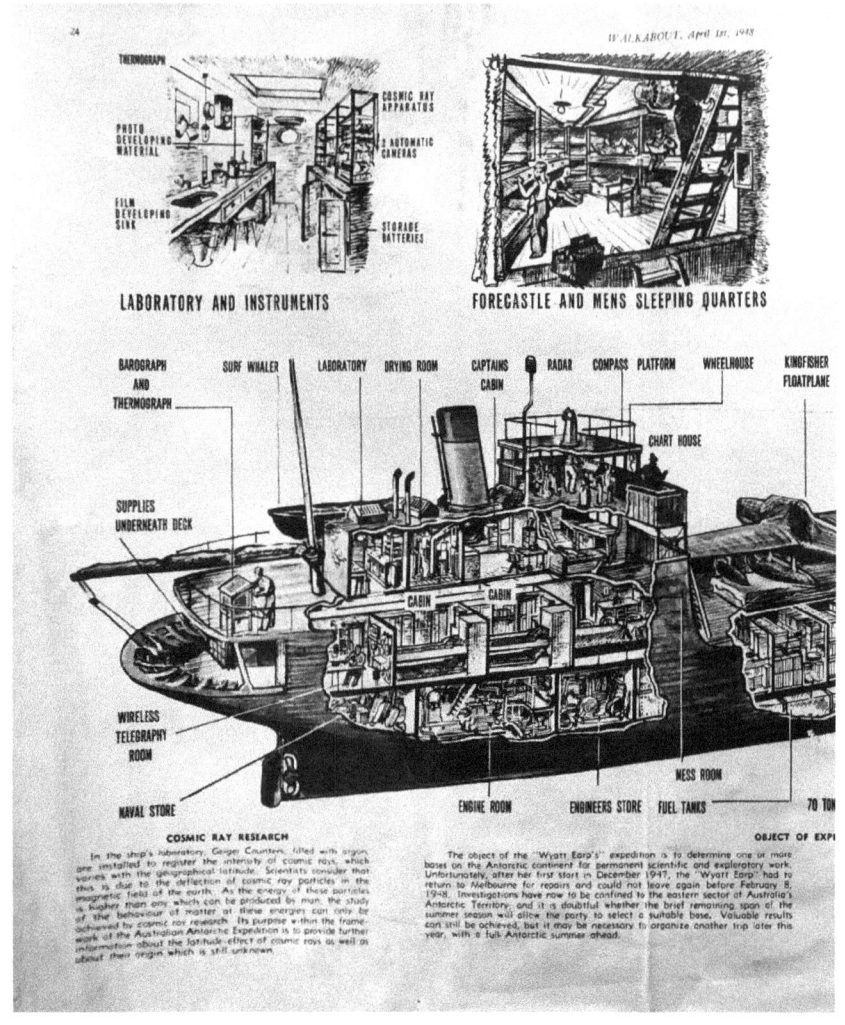

Details of refitted HMAS *Wyatt Earp*. Courtesy: Naval History Section—Sea Power Centre.

Re-Naming of HMAS "Wongala"

1. HMAS "WONGALA" is at present fitting out at Adelaide for the purpose of proceeding to the Antarctic later this year on behalf of the Australian National Antarctic Research Expedition. Observing ship achieved an international reputation for similar work as the "Wyatt Earp" it has been decided that it is re-named accordingly.

Chapter 3 — War service and Sea Scouts

2. The new name is to be brought into use forthwith.[27]

The refit did not go smoothly. It was delayed by industrial disputes. The shipwrights refused to work with dilutee shipwrights (those who did not pay union fees to the Shipwrights' Association). At one stage there was a suggestion that the expedition would be postponed because of the delays. The crew for the forthcoming voyage came on board while the ship was still on the slipway.

Tally Band, HMAS *Wyatt Earp*. Courtesy: Naval History Section—Sea Power Centre.

HMAS *Wyatt Earp* was, in the event, recommissioned on 17 November 1947, at Port Adelaide under the command of Commander K. E. Oom. Sir Douglas and Lady Mawson visited the ship on 9 December, Sir Douglas having been well acquainted with her before this major work (not yet completed even as she departed for sea). On 11 December pupils and staff from Ethelton School presented the vessel with a Blue Ensign. Because of the delays there was insufficient time for sea trials, resulting in plenty of problems on the Antarctic voyages. HMAS *Wyatt Earp* left Port Adelaide for Williamstown in Melbourne on 13 December 1947. The work still to be carried out could be done while she loaded stores and the plane at Williamstown Dockyard.

The Second World War was over. The Australian Government's concerns about a presence in the Antarctic had resurfaced. The long years of waiting were over and HMAS *Wyatt Earp* would shortly be on her way south again.

Endnotes

1. *Recorder* (Port Pirie), 19 January 1939, p. 4.
2. 'Report of the Ellsworth Antarctic Flight Expedition, 1938–39' from Sir Hubert Wilkins, to the Minister, Department of External Affairs, Commonwealth of Australia. Australian Archives, A1838, 1495/1 ANNEX D.
3. *Sydney Morning Herald*, 7 August 1939, p. 12.
4. *Kalgoorlie Miner*, 10 February 1939, p. 1.
5. *Singleton Argus*, 6 April 1939, p. 4.
6. *Advocate* (Burnie, Tas.) 11 March 1939, p. 9.
7. NAA: A6006, 1939/08/03, p. 1.
8. NAA: A6006, 1939/08/03, p. 3. NB: In 1939 it was practice to record a Cabinet decision with an annotation on the file.
9. This word for 'boomerang' is from the Yuwibara (also Yuwi, Yuibera) language spoken in the Mackay area of Queensland.
10. www.navy.gov.au/sites/default/files/documents/Commonwealth_Naval_Orders_1948.pdf, 21 November 1939, p. 155.
11. www.navy.gov.au/hmas-wyatt-earp
12. *Sydney Morning Herald*, 6 April 1940, p. 22.
13. Personal conversation author with J. I. Moore
14. From article 'The Navy in South Australia' sent by Commander B. K. Gorringe to the Adelaide *Advertiser* in a letter dated 18 March 1994. The author of the article is not known. Attached to email from Naval History Section - Sea Power Centre.
15. *Advertiser* (Adelaide), 5 March 1945, p. 6.
16. *Advertiser* (Adelaide), 12 February 1947, p. 10
17. *Advertiser* (Adelaide), 21 March 1946, p. 7.
18. Philip Law, *The Antarctic Voyage of HMAS Wyatt Earp*, Allen & Unwin, 1995, p. 6.
19. Law, p. 6.
20. *Advertiser* (Adelaide), 12 February 1947, p. 10.
21. *News* (Adelaide), 29 April 1947, p. 1.
22. Cook, W.F., 'HMAS Wyatt Earp - Antarctic Research 1947–1948', *Naval Historical Review*, December 1978.
23. *Advertiser* (Adelaide), 4 June 1947, p. 3.
24. Cook, W.F., 'HMAS Wyatt Earp - Antarctic Research 1947–1948', *Naval Historical Review*, December 1978. Cook was responsible for keeping the expedition journal and in 2015 his son donated the journal and other memorabilia to the Australian National Maritime Museum.
25. Hansard, House of Representatives, 3 June 1947.
26. Documents held in file "Wyatt Earp" by Naval History Section - Sea Power Centre.
27. Letter dated 5 August 1947 in files, 'Wyatt Earp', held by Naval History Section - Sea Power Centre.

WYATT EARP: The little ship with many names

A fine day in Antarctic waters off Young Island, in the Balleny Group, in February 1948. Courtesy: Naval History Section — Sea Power Centre.

Chapter 3 War service and Sea Scouts

The stunning scenery at Whaler's Bay, Deception Island, 7 November 2019, would have changed little since *Wyatt Earp* visited in the 1930s. Courtesy: Margaret Mortimer.

(78343) Souvenir from Cape Town 1933. Courtesy: Magnus Johannessen's photo album, Romsdalsmuseet, Norway

WYATT EARP: The little ship with many names

The Bell from *Fanefjord* and HMAS *Wyatt Earp*.

The bell is inscribed with the *Fanefjord*'s details on one side and HMAS *Wyatt Earp*'s on the other side.

© Jonothan Davis. Courtesy: Australian Antarctic Division. The bell is currently on loan to the South Australian Museum.

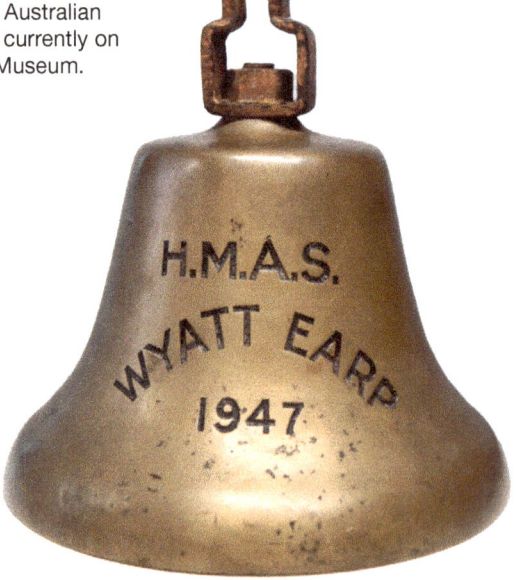

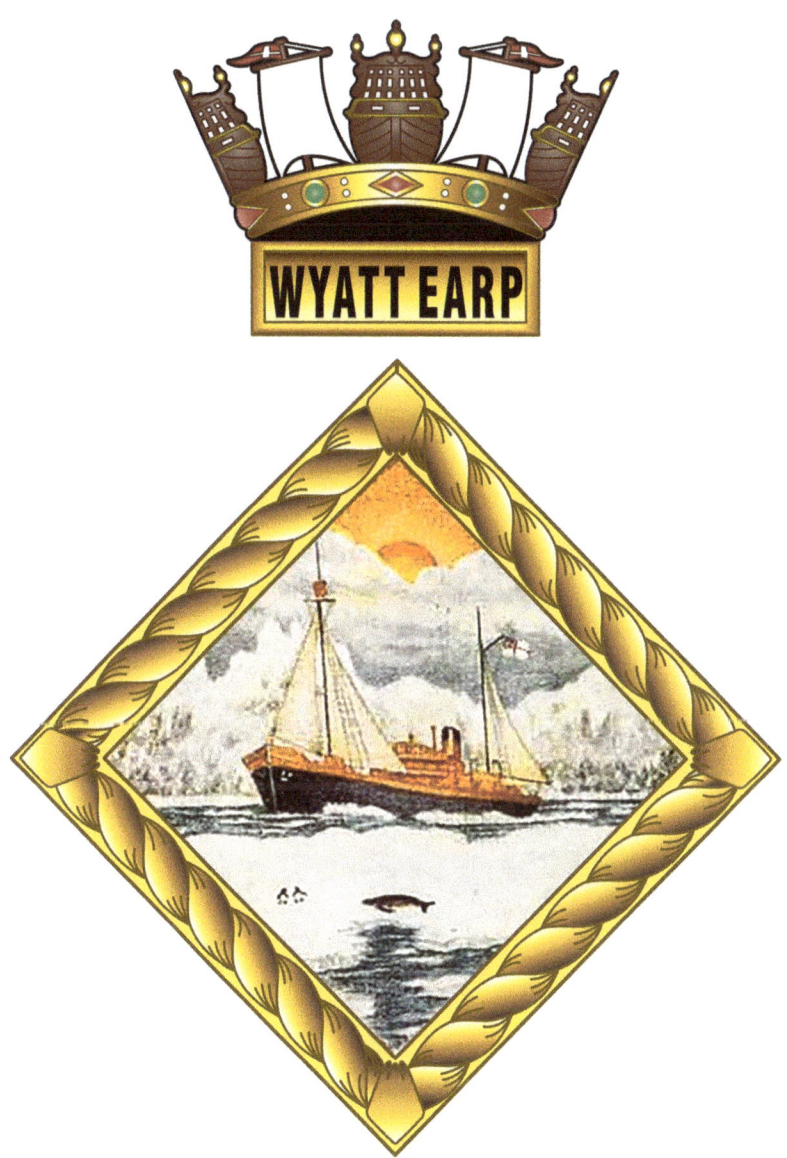

Label pasted in the title page of ANARE HMAS Wyatt Earp's log kept by the First Lieutenant, Lieutenant Commander W. F. Cook. Courtesy: Naval History Section—Sea Power Centre.

Chapter 4

HMAS Wyatt Earp

'Twerp' and the first Australian National Antarctic Research Expedition

Lieutenant Commander W. F. Cook was First Lieutenant of HMAS *Wyatt Earp* for the first Australian National Antarctic Research Expedition in 1947–1948. He began his account of the voyage by writing: '*Wyatt Earp* is such an improbable name for one of His Majesty's Australian ships that people often doubt her existence. She, of course, delighted in the nickname of the *Twerp*'.[1](Cook/NHR)

Why was the *Twerp* heading south on behalf of Australia so many years after Sir Douglas Mawson's 1929–31 BANZARE (British Australian (and) New Zealand Antarctic Research Expeditions) voyages? Both the Depression and the Second World War had meant Australia's objectives and resources were focussed in other areas, and in other ways, but, as seen earlier, Mawson and Wilkins both kept advocating for permanent Australian bases on the Antarctic mainland and at Macquarie Island and Heard Island. They believed there should be a physical presence on the Continent, in order to support Australia's territorial claims and to continue the exploration and science started earlier. With the Government's purchase of the (now) HMAS *Wyatt Earp*, transport was available. The plans and objects of the Expedition are outlined in the previous chapter and so the naval ship, equipped with a suitable aircraft as suggested by the interdepartmental committee, was about to head south for the Antarctic.

Commander Karl Oom was Captain of the *Wyatt Earp*. Head of the RAN Hydrographic Office, he had been a member of Mawson's 1930–31 BANZARE voyage. He had extensive surveying and cartographic experience and was described as a 'self-assured, imperturbable and splendid seaman, with an impish sense of humour; in other regards Cook found him an enigmatic man who kept his own counsel.'[2]

Philip Law, a 35 year old Melbourne University academic, was the Chief Scientific Officer and Group Captain Stuart Campbell was Chief Executive Officer of the newly formed ANARE. Campbell, like Oom, had sailed with Mawson—as chief pilot on the two BANZARE voyages, 1929–30 and 1930–31. It was not originally planned that he should go on this voyage but he joined *Wyatt Earp* for the second voyage.

The crew chosen for the Antarctic voyage joined HMAS *Wyatt Earp* while she was still on the slipway in Port Adelaide undergoing reconstruction, repairs and extensions to ensure she was seaworthy and to make life more comfortable for the crew.

HMAS *Wyatt Earp* at Williamstown Dockyard, Melbourne, December 1947, loading more supplies before the first ANARE voyage. Courtesy: Naval History Section—Sea Power Centre.

Chapter 4					HMAS Wyatt Earp

HMAS *Wyatt Earp* departs Melbourne for first ANARE voyage, December 1947. Courtesy: Naval History Section—Sea Power Centre.

HMAS *Wyatt Earp* tied up alongside HMAS Gascoyne at Williamstown, c. December 1947/January 1948. Courtesy: Naval History Section—Sea Power Centre.

Oom's 'Report of Proceedings' states the ship was scheduled to depart Port Adelaide at 0900 on 12 December, but this was delayed to noon the following day by the contractors and followed by a further change to 1715 on 13 December. The causes: 'Difficulties in stowing the aircraft and motor boat. Despite repeated demands, boat chocks were only supplied at the last minute and when the ship finally slipped much work still in hand.' (Oom).

The three-and-a-half day voyage to Melbourne, to finish some of the modifications and to load more supplies, was not pleasant. It was really the sea trial they had not had time for before departure and:

> With head winds and rough seas all the way to Melbourne, it was a very wet trip. Water came in everywhere; into the mess decks forward and down into the gyro which it put out of action—into the cabins and wardroom aft; and all this necessitated bailing. A steering breakdown was thrown in for good luck (or bad luck)! (Cook/NHR)

Almost all repairs were done by 19 December and the ship, almost fully loaded with stores and fuel, sailed at 1342 for Hobart. At 1417, still in Port Phillip Bay and less than an hour after departure, the main engines had to be stopped, owing to a defective control. They were restarted at 1547 in order to return alongside. The engine control was improved and at 1605 the ship headed for Port Phillip Heads, passing through at 2300:

> During 20th December a strong gale from East contradicted storm warnings that gales could be expected from the West. During the Afternoon the wind veered to E.S.E. with gusts up to 55 m.p.h. accompanied by driving rain and spray. Ship's way was almost stopped and due to fully loaded condition the ship's movement was extremely violent and uncomfortable. Water poured in through the ship's side into after accommodation, through fore decking into accommodation for'ard and through bridge structure into Chart Room and C.O's cabin. (Oom)

HMAS *Wyatt Earp* arrived in Hobart three days and six hours after leaving Melbourne, 'secured alongside Elizabeth Street Pier' at 1945 on 22 December, and immediately the shipwright contractor was on board, and re-caulking commenced to try and make her watertight. In Melbourne a

Navy Public Relations Officer told the *Herald* that 'as no particulars of the damage had been given in the Navy signal, it was evidently not serious'.[3] He went on to say the ship 'would not be allowed to proceed on the voyage to the Antarctic unless absolutely seaworthy'.

The following day in Hobart, under the heading 'Wyatt Earp Buffeted by Fierce Gale', Commander Oom was reported as saying that:

> Water poured through leaks in all the upper works of the ship ... It flooded cabins, damaging clothes and personal effects, and made the task of the cook so difficult that on Monday it was possible only to serve soup for luncheon.[4]

More repairs, final loading of fresh food and topping up fuel was completed in time to allow *Wyatt Earp* to depart at 0700 on Christmas Day for the compass adjustment, a necessary action for all ships at that time.[5] Almost immediately there was engine trouble, with salt water emulsifying the lubricating oil. Returning to the wharf, to drop the Compass Adjuster, the main engine-controlling mechanism jammed again and the ship hit the pier, without causing damage, and was brought to a stop by head and stern lines.

> So we just hung around till the engine room assessed and adjusted that defect. What an anticlimax! We had done everything in our power to get the ship away from Hobart before Christmas and here we are broken down alongside a wharf just as Christmas Dinner is announced. What gloom! The gloom lasted till after the evening meal when the Captain prescribed champagne cocktails and we sang with Phil Law's accordion and danced and skylarked till about 3 a.m. (Cook/NHR)

Finally, on 26 December 1947, at 1315, *Wyatt Earp* left Hobart, via the D'Entrecasteaux Channel but:

> The encouraging weather forecast was soon discovered to be misleading as immediately the ship cleared Cape Bruny at 1915 the wind increased from the West and the barometer commenced to fall rapidly. At Midnight the wind had reached Force 9 from the West with ship hove-to to the Westward of Eddystone Rock.

> It was discouraging to find the sea again entering accommodation aft through the ships side and this was believed to be due to the heavily laden condition of the ship with its violent movement in the heavy sea producing undue strain on the superstructure. (Oom)

Cook put it simply: 'As she rolled, the planks worked, and the water came in.' On 28 December they had a following wind and full sail was set, making about eight knots. But another gale, from the south-west, gave very unpleasant conditions during the night and next morning with the aft accommodation requiring constant bailing. The steering gear gave way and they stopped for repairs. The Engineer Officer reported that the amount of water leaking through the holding-down bolts of the engine seemed to be increasing. On 30 December engines were stopped for another repair and 'The 'Chippy', the 'Buffer' & I went over the side on a stage & plugged, caulked & canvassed a considerable stretch of the starboard side abreast of the W/T office & Bosn's cabin. Pretty cold work, as the water kept washing up to our knees.' (Cook/ANMM)

> The barometer continued its alarming downward plunge to 972 mbs. until 0200 on 31st. As the wind had been continually East during this fall it points to the unusual fact of a deep depression moving rapidly on a Southerly course.
>
> After a long wait with the barometer at 972 mbs. level wind increased to gale force from the West and after being hove-to until 2000 ships course 220° was resumed. (Oom)

Oom reports that on 1 January 1948, for the first time since leaving Adelaide, they had fine weather. They stopped for further repairs to the ship's side and received a signal from A.C.N.B. (Acting Chief Naval Board) ordering their immediate return to Williamstown.[6] The weather continued fine with following winds and, after an exchange of signals, they had an uneventful return to Melbourne, arriving on 7 January. They docked at Station Pier and next day unloaded the aircraft and perishable stores and proceeded to the Alfred Graving Dock (dry dock) at Williamstown, where they stayed until 28 January.

Some of the highlights of the next five weeks, apart from six days leave to each watch, were the dockyard stiffening up the engine bed, refitting the main and the auxiliary engines, taking out the shaft, renewing the stern bushes, taking off and replacing the sheathing in order to survey the hull, replacing part of the stern post, re-rigging the steering, caulking the upper deck and ship's side and doing many other small jobs. (Cook/NHR)

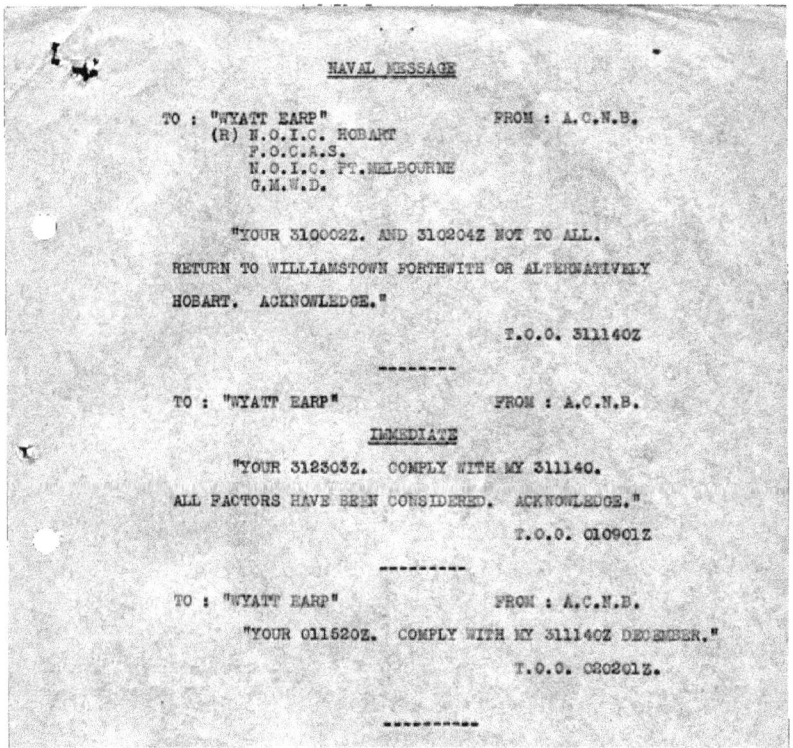

Copy of Naval Messages including 'RETURN TO WILLIAMSTOWN FORTHWITH' attached to the 'Report of Proceedings', Australian War Memorial, File AWM78/372/1

Various newspapers reported the return of the *Wyatt Earp* to Melbourne for urgent repairs. The Minister for the Navy, W. J. F. Riordan, stated 'there was no possibility of the Antarctic research expedition being postponed until next year because of the damage.'[7] Another paper added to the confusion about what was happening by stating: 'Meanwhile, it is understood negotiations are going on in the United States and Britain for a bigger wooden ship to replace the Wyatt Earp, which now apparently is regarded as being too small.'[8] Headline news in northern New South Wales was 'Search for Ship to Replace Wyatt Earp', saying 'Reason for the negotiations is that the Wyatt Earp, being less than 300 tons, is not big enough to land an expedition with a year's provisions in the Antarctic. Her speed is slow for the nature of her work.'[9] And *Wyatt Earp* had not even arrived back in Melbourne on this date!

Meanwhile the Chief Executive Officer of the newly formed Australian National Antarctic Research Expedition (ANARE), Group Captain Stuart Campbell, had gone to Heard Island on the LST 3501 (Landing Ship, Tank, later HMAS *Labuan*) to set up the first Australian scientific research station there. The plan was that *Wyatt Earp* would call at Heard Island on her way back from the Antarctic and collect Campbell at the end of the summer. On Friday 2 January 1948, LST 3501, which had been on a visit to the Kerguelen Islands on its way back to Australia, returned hurriedly to Heard Island after receiving a signal sending them back to Heard Island to see if Campbell wanted to return to Australia with them, as the damaged *Wyatt Earp* was currently returning to Williamstown for repairs:

> It appeared likely that the Wyatt Earp might not be able to call at Heard Island and pick me up as arranged, and Dixon was to return to Heard Island, advise me of these facts, and see if I wanted to come back to Australia.
>
> This was a difficult one. My first reaction is to stay here and take a chance on being picked up later on. Even if they cant pick me up, I won't mind particularly, I can find lots to keep me busy and interested here for a year. (Campbell)

After much thought overnight, Campbell made the difficult decision that he should return with LST 3501 to Australia. They sailed on 4 January, arriving back in Williamstown on 18 January, by which time repairs on *Wyatt Earp* had begun, although a strike by the Painters' and Dockers' Union again delayed her return to sea. The *Advocate* (Burnie) noted this stating that, if the men returned to work on Monday (19 January), 'repair and refitting of the ship could be completed within two weeks. After that about four days would be required for trials and final preparation.'[10] The same article also noted that a 'new schedule for *Wyatt Earp* will be discussed by the committee after the return of the expedition's leader (G. Capt. Campbell) in L.S.T. 3501 at the weekend.'

The Executive Planning Committee met in Canberra on 23 January 1948. Philip Law as well as Stuart Campbell and Karl Oom all attended. Campbell announced his intention to accompany *Wyatt Earp*. A number of matters relating to scientific work were sorted out; the question of watchkeeping was raised and agreed it should be left to the Captain; and because of lack of space the Chairman of the Committee ruled out taking an observer from the French polar exploration organisation. 'Oom was left in absolute command of the expedition, although Campbell would clearly be able, as the leader of ANARE, to exert considerable influence on any decisions apart from those concerning safety of the ship.' (Law, p. 75)

On 4 February speed and anchoring trials were carried out in Port Phillip:

> For further trials at sea ship slipped at 0700 on 6th February with dockyard officers on board and passed through the Heads at midday. After taking on board some heavy seas in the Rip moderate conditions were encountered outside and course was set to obtain maximum amount of movement. Main Engine was stopped at 1800 as the level of Engine Room bilge water had risen above safely level because all bilge suctions had become blocked. After suctions had been cleared Main Engine could not be restarted until 2200 when course was resumed. (Oom)

Wyatt Earp departed again, finally, from Melbourne on 8 February. Cook reports:

> We had good weather with all the strong winds abaft the beam for almost a week. Thereafter we had four days of bad rolling but continued to make good southing mostly with our sails set. As the temperature dropped our excitement rose. We had a wonderful display of Aurora Australis on 14 February when in about 55° south.

And bad rolling it was! Oom's report explains:

On 13th February (53° 16′ S., 144° 10′ E.), good progress was maintained with assistance of sails to steady the ship against the wind which continued at full gale force, however at 2200, after two violent rolls of 60° or more, course was altered to W.S.W. and speed reduced. Heavy rolling increases the leaks into after accommodation.

The first icebergs were sighted on 18 February and Campbell described the thrill, even for those who had seen them before:

They were all around us, at least six of them. Huge flat slabs of gleaming white ice with vertical sides rising 150 feet sheet out of the sea. Along the waterline are huge caverns in which the sea boils and foams as the surge runs in and out. Here and there the sides are split in deep V-shaped crevasses, out which shines a pale iridescent flow of the deepest blue. Two of the bergs were at least five miles long and the others between one half and two miles.

Oom's Report says that 'the wind abated to gale force' on 20 February and they resumed their course to the south among the pack ice, trying to find an open lead. There were many penguins, seals and whales about. The next day they got within 30 miles of the coast but the ice blocked their way and the weather made launching the plane impossible. They cleared the pack and moved east with more bad weather.

'WYATT EARP' with her straight stem and small displacement, 725 tons deep loads, (S.Y. 'DISCOVERY' 1900 tons) and awkwardness in turning to Starboard in a confined space, is not a good ship for forcing a passage through pack ice. (Oom)

As noted previously, Stuart Campbell had been an expedition member on Mawson's BANZARE expeditions, on *Discovery I* in 1929–30 and 1930–31, while Karl Oom had been the hydrographer/cartographer on the second voyage. Both had considerable experience in the ice. In *South Latitude*, F. D. Ommanney, a marine biologist on board *Discovery II*, when telling the story of both *Wyatt Earp* and *Discovery II* trying to reach the Bay of Whales in the Ross Sea in January 1936, says: 'We had the advantage of power but the *Wyatt Earp* was on the whole far better adapted for pushing through ice since she had a stout wooden hull, as against our shell of steel.'[11] Not everyone thought *Wyatt Earp* was unsuitable for work in the ice.

Wherever they tried, ice blocked their way and, when in the ice, they had to stop during the few hours of darkness. On 27 February they gave up trying to reach the coast and headed for the Balleny Islands. Although discovered by Captain John Balleny in 1839, even by 1948 there were very few recorded landings mainly due to steep cliffs and a lack of landing places. Little information existed about the Islands. *Discovery II*, however, had made use of her trip to the Bay of Whales in 1936 when, while returning with Lincoln Ellsworth and Hubert Wilkins, a running survey was made producing the first accurate chart of the area.

Travelling through heavy snow, *Wyatt Earp* reached Young Island, in the Balleny group, late on the afternoon of 28 February. The ship stopped, awaiting an improvement in the weather. Philip Law called 29 February 'the most active day of our voyage up until to then.' (p.94). Hoping to collect some rock specimens, he was part of the group that, still too rough for the motor boat, launched a whaler and rowed about two miles to a little beach. Campbell, Law and Wallace landed in knee deep water (or in Law's case thigh deep which filled his knee boots!). However, it was impossible to make the boat fast or pull her up on the land. They had a long cold and tiring row back to the ship. According to Law:

> The coast was forbidding in the extreme. The highest point on the island (Borradaile), halfway along the western coast, was later estimated from the ship to be 1,250 feet high. Most of the rest of the island was found to be 500 to 1,000 feet, and along the entire coastline, apart from the north-western tip, high ice cliffs plunged vertically into the sea. This day, however, with cloud at less than 1,000 feet, much of this was not visible to us. (Law, p. 94)

The wind blew erratically with gusts of hurricane force and thick snow. On 4 March the day was clear, sunny and calm, only the second clear day since 14 February! As weather permitted, *Wyatt Earp* spent until 6 March either sheltering or conducting running surveys, something Captain and Hydrographer Oom was particularly keen on.

A running survey entails steaming parallel and close to the shore on a steady course and at a steady speed and taking a set of bearings of prominent points, a sounding, and a radar range of the nearest land every two minutes. By correlating all this data a reasonably accurate picture for the part of the world is obtained. (Cook/NHR)

Coast of Buckle Island, Balleny Islands on 6 February 2006. Typical of the coast with few if any landing places and steep cliffs. Photo: Trish Burgess.

All the islands appeared to be similarly inhospitable with no suitable landing places found:

> Although it is possible to land at least on Buckle and Borradaile Islands in favourable weather, it would in all cases necessitate an ice mountaineering climb to get from these landing spots to the top of the island. It would be necessary to traverse heavily crevassed areas and steep slopes where the danger of avalanches would be very great. (Campbell)

Pack ice was very close to Young and Buckle islands and it was impossible to get within 14 miles of Sturge Island. There was thick snow and low visibility and, with no signs of improvement, they set a course west for Commonwealth Bay. On 10 March, with decreasing visibility and in amongst loose drift ice, they stopped, but remained rolling heavily in a short steep sea:

> We are only about 40 miles from land but can't go pushing in amongst the ice in this weather. The Wyatt Earp is not a very good ice ship; she is too light and has too blunt a bow to crack anything but the very lightest ice. When we hit even a small old floe we take a very solid jar and it is doubtful if she would stand much of that sort of work. She does not manoeuvre very well either and is awkward in turning to starboard. (Campbell)

On 11 March they were stopped by a 'solid wall of pack ice stretching indefinitely Southward and to East and West.' (Oom)

> On 13 March the Mertz glacier ice tongue was entered to procure a lee from the swell in order to lower the Kingfisher for a reconnaissance flight. The plane was hoisted out at 1400 and after two flights over the glacier, the latter with the official photographer, Mr. Le Guay, the plane was hoisted inboard at 1600 and dismantled.
>
> ...
>
> Experience has proved that the 'WYATT EARP' is too small a ship to carry an aircraft such as the 'Kingfisher' for operational use from the ship as the movement of the ship is so lively that perfectly calm shelter has to be found before working the plane. In addition, once assembled, the aircraft is difficult to house safely against the ship's violent movement in a seaway. (Oom)

Campbell's Diary expanded on the problems relating to the aircraft:

> The First Lieut. decided to get the motor boat out first—a seemingly impossible task, as she was stowed inside the rigging and underneath the wing of the aircraft, and it was hard to see how she could be juggled out safely hanging from the end of a derrick. She Wasn't!! We put a hole in the side, very early in the proceedings, and it was decided that that idea was no good.

> With a ship like the Wyatt Earp, there is little real need to lower a boat for flying operations, but I decided we'd put the whaler over just in case the aircraft wouldn't start or needed a tow, and to act as a tender for changing passengers. (Campbell)

The plane was unloaded and took off successfully. The flight confirmed there was no way through the ice for *Wyatt Earp* to reach the coast so it was decided, after skirting a big concentration of icebergs, some ten miles long, to head north and for Macquarie Island. In his diary Campbell makes some comments about the ship:

> The days slip by with remarkable rapidity now: just another instance of how quickly one becomes accustomed to a new routine and ceases to look ahead. In the early stages of the voyage, these days at sea with no variation were boredom, but now one hardly notices them go by. Nevertheless, this ship is far too small for even reasonable comfort and privacy on a long voyage. Now after 2 months, one is used to the confinement which seems less than earlier, but after 4 months, it would begin to pall.
>
> If the Wyatt Earp goes down again, she should have a much reduced crew and the Scientific Staff all be called upon to do ship's duties. It should also be run as a Merchant Vessel or Yacht, and not as a Naval Vessel under the Operational Command of the Navy Board. But I'm afraid she really belongs to a past era of Antarctic Exploration when requirements were simple and scientific aims not very complex. To-day, we need complicated equipment, specialised personnel and room to employ them in.
>
> I believe that the day is past when any really useful work can be done by a vessel such as the Wyatt Earp, unless it be confined to surveying by small shore parties. She could be used for a private expedition, but not for a Government one, which necessarily has to be launched on a much larger scale. (Campbell)

They left the ice behind, started writing letters home to post from Macquarie Island and, with some fine and sunny days, interspersed with the odd gale, they anchored in Buckles Bay at Macquarie Island at noon on 20 March. LST 3501 was there before them, busy landing the scientific party who would be the first to spend the winter at the newly established Macquarie Island ANARE station, which has operated continuously since. The Captain of LST 3501 (Lieutenant Commander George Dixon) sent a LCVP (Landing Craft Vehicles, Personnel) with a message offering the facilities of his ship to those on *Wyatt Earp*. '"Facilities" of course, in this context mean just two things; a hot shower and beer in the wardroom. After lunch a large party of us went across and took advantage of the first part of the offer.' (Campbell). Macquarie Island lived up to expectations as far as weather was concerned (records suggests that it rains 315 days out of 365) and a party went ashore in driving rain.

Wyatt Earp spent several days in Buckles Bay, with all on board relaxing slightly and some people spending time on the island. Phillip Law commented: 'Ashore at Macquarie Island I was a new man—alert and energetic, with a huge appetite and able to call on completely different, deeper sleep. I enjoyed the change immensely.' (Law, p. 119) The ship drew fresh water from the LST and was ready to sail on 23 March but weather conditions— wind gusts up to 70 MPH and more driving rain—did not permit departure. *Wyatt Earp* departed Buckles Bay at 0600 on 24 March, the weather having improved slightly but with a rain squall passing over.

> As we cleared the lee of the island to the north we ran into a screaming westerly. Macquarie Island is a visible manifestation (together with the Bishop and Clerk Islands to the south and the Judge and Clerk Islands to the north) of a submarine mountain chain which rises very steeply from depths of thousands of fathoms. The long unhindered westerly swell of the Southern Ocean builds up alarmingly over this relatively shallow shelf and the seas in a gale must be seen to be believed. Once having committed ourselves it was safer to continue on rather than attempt to turn, and the next two hours were in my estimation the most dangerous of the whole. We crossed the mile wide shelf at a speed of one knot with engine revolutions on for seven. I wrote 'It was fantastic that the old ship could live through such water without taking dangerous amounts on board. We rolled like a log, pitched, tossed, yawed, rose to incredible heights on crests and

plunged to abysmal depths in the troughs. She did everything but stand vertical although once or twice she tried her damndest. Most of the time one felt like a buckjump rider expecting to be pitched off or to feel the mount fall under you. It was exciting to say the least of it'. (Cook/NHR)

Philip Law, quoting his diary, wrote:

The seas were as high as any we had seen. The *Wyatt Earp* would climb to the towering crest of one, then plunge with sickening velocity—faster than the fastest lift—to the trough, where she would bury her bows in the next swell, before shaking free of the engulfing water and laboriously climbing the steep wall ahead. The accelerations on the downward path would be greater than 'g' (the acceleration due to gravity), for the upthrust of the passing wave under the stern would tip the ship and propel its bows downwards so that one's feet would leave the deck. (In bed at night in such waves the bunks falls away from beneath one's body and one catches up with it with a jolt at the bottom of the drop.) The ship made a maximum speed of only 2½ knots throughout that day. (Law, p. 120.)

The Captain noted in his 'Report of Proceedings' that 'Departure was soon found to be premature as the barometer continued to rise all day and the full gale from W.S.W. permitted very slight progress. Two hours were taken to cross the two mile wide shallow shelf, extending North from Macquarie, against a very steep and heavy sea.' (Oom) While Cook noted:

The weather did improve later that day and the next day they were left with a huge swell and rain and mist in the morning but were able to make a steady 7 knots. On 26 March, Good Friday, conditions were much the same and on 27 March they had sun almost all day. On 28 March they set all sail and made 8 knots part of the time until a wind change forced them to reduce sail and speed. 29 March was similar and at 0438 on 30 March, on a 'beautifully quiet & calm morning' Eddystone Light was sighted and 'we were "bang on" for a good landfall!' (Cook/NMAA).

Cook continued:

> Bass Strait has to be seen to be believed today! Most beautifully calm!! Lovely sun, cloudless sky, no swell at all, and a light breeze from the NNE—ideal conditions—and yet the radio tells us that during the past 48 hours at least 2 ships have limped into Melbourne battered by bad weather in the Strait.

On 31 March *Wyatt Earp* passed through the Rip into Port Phillip Bay about 1730 and they anchored off St Leonards, on the Bellarine Peninsula, east of Geelong. The Navy had made arrangements for an official welcome next morning! Cook (ANMM) recorded: 'Most of us went to the trouble of bathing & dressing for dinner', ... 'an excellent dinner, & over port & coffee ... we fell to speech making (of a sort!!)'. Although Law observed that (p. 122) 'All of us were very disappointed. ... In fact there was almost a mutiny among a few men, who kicked around a proposal to take one of the ship's boats and row ashore. Instead a party of considerable proportions developed, continuing all night.' *Wyatt Earp* came alongside Station Pier at 0915 on 1 April 1948, welcomed back by family, friends, members of the press and photographers.

The Melbourne *Age* under the headline 'Wyatt Earp—Adventures in the Antarctic' reported that after a 7,000 mile voyage, Group Captain Stuart Campbell said 'the trip had been completely successful. Highlights of the voyage were:

> A survey of the Balleny Islands, which were discovered in 1839 and had not been visited since.[12]
>
> Intense cosmic-ray and meteorological observations, the results of which might not be known for some months.
>
> The regular reception of meteorological reports from Japanese whaling vessels, but close secrecy by whalers from other countries.
>
> The fitness of the crew ...
>
> And a mishap in Port Phillip Bay early yesterday, when Group Captain Campbell spent 10 minutes in the icy sea. . . .

> One other fact of interest that might be included among the 'highlights' was the birth of two healthy kittens to Mimi on the very edge of the Antarctic continent.'[13]

The article quoted Group Captain Campbell speaking about the ship:

> The Wyatt Earp had behaved splendidly throughout. The engines and the hull had been 100 per cent.
>
> 'But there is no doubt that we want a roomier and more modern ship for future exploration,' he added. 'Here we were cramped and somewhat uncomfortable. An eight months' stay in the Antarctic in such conditions would have been almost intolerable.'

Mr Stuart Campbell was quoted again the following month, in a report in the *Age*, under the heading 'Wyatt Earp to Go South Again':

> Efforts to obtain a new ship for the Australian Antarctic expedition have not been successful, and the Wyatt Earp will probably make the trip south again.
>
> This was stated by Mr Stuart Campbell, leader of the Australian Antarctic expedition, during an address to the monthly luncheon of the Federal Institute of Accountants yesterday.
>
> Inquiries have been made all over the world for a larger ship, but a suitable craft was not available, he said.
>
> Ship-building yards in Britain and other countries had been approached, but they had orders for five years ahead. The same applied in Australia.
>
> Mr Stuart Campbell defended the seaworthiness of the Wyatt Earp, and said she was a good ship for the job, apart from her smallness.[14]

Despite Campbell's comments *Wyatt Earp* was paid off on 30 June 1948, and lay idle at Williamstown Dockyard for three years:

> Was the voyage successful? Did it meet its objectives or did factors beyond human control cause damage, which delayed the start so long that they missed the optimum time/weather for getting through the pack ice to the continent? Did modifications to the ship cause her to roll more than previously, and sustain leaks and other damage greater than on previous voyages?

Wyatt Earp had made four Antarctic voyages with Lincoln Ellsworth. Perhaps his Norwegian crews were used to big seas and rolling ships?

The main objective—to find a suitable ice-free site with landing access on the Antarctic continent on which to establish Australia's first permanent base—was not achieved. The expedition could not reach the mainland. But despite this, the voyage achieved much of the scientific work set out in the program, even though Phillip Law commented: 'The program for the *Wyatt Earp* voyage was ambitious.[15]

The first ANARE expedition raised the profile of Australia's Antarctic territorial claims in the eyes of the public and the need for such expeditions. Newspapers played a large role in this with constant stories and quotes from people such as Sir Douglas Mawson and Sir Hubert Wilkins, already Australian Antarctic heroes. New ships for Antarctic work were leased and bases built and today Australia's territorial claim is acknowledged. *Wyatt Earp* played a very large role in this.

Endnotes

1   Captain W. F. Cook's article, 'HMAS Wyatt Earp - Antarctic Research 1947–1948', in *Naval Historical Review*, December 1978.
    Apart from the above reference and newspaper articles, there are four main sources of information for this chapter:

   The two 'Report of Proceedings' by the Commanding Officer of HMAS *Wyatt Earp*, Commander Karl Oom, dated 8 January 1948 and 1 April 1948; held by the Australian War Memorial File AWM78/372/1;

   Philip Law's book, *The Antarctic Voyage of 'HMAS Wyatt Earp'*, published by Allen & Unwin in 1995;

   Group Captain Stuart Campbell's handwritten diaries held in the National Archives of Australia under NAA: P1557, 4 Item 840298;

   Transcript of, then, Lieutenant Commander W. F. Cook's *Journal of the Voyage of HMAS Wyatt Earp (Australian National Antarctic Research Expedition, 1947–1948)* held by the Australian National Maritime Museum Collection 00054702.

    Where quoted in this chapter, they are referenced as Oom, Law, Campbell, Cook/ANMM and Cook/NHR.

2   J.S.Compton, 'Oom, Karl Erik (1904–1972)', *Australian Dictionary of Biography*, Australian National Centre of Biography, Australian National University, http://adb.anu.edu.au/biography/oom-karl-erik-11309/text20187. accessed online 4 February 2020.
3   *Herald* (Melbourne), 23 December 1947, p. 3.
4   *Advocate* (Burnie), 24 December 1947, p. 1.
5   Compass adjustment: After major structural and or equipment changes a ship's own unique magnetic signature may change. It is necessary to check the magnetic steering compass and if necessary compensate for any bias the ship's magnetism causes to it. This is done with small magnets placed in small compartments in the binnacle housing the steering compass. From Commodore John Compton AM RAN Retd.
6   Australian War Memorial AWM78,372/1
7   *The Age* (Melbourne), 13 January 1948, p. 2.
8   *Chronicle* (Adelaide), 8 January 1948, p. 4.
9   *Tweed Daily* (Murwillumbah), 6 January 1948, p. 1.
10 *Advocate* (Burnie), 15 January 1948, p. 5.
11 F.D. Ommanney, *South Latitude*, Longmans, Green and Co., 1938, p. 190.
12 Incorrect, as *Discovery II* spent time there doing survey and scientific work en route from the Ross Sea to Melbourne, after rescuing Lincoln Ellsworth. See Chapter 2.
13 *Age* (Melbourne), 2 April 1948, p. 3.
14 *The Age*, 26 May 1948, p. 2.
15 Phillip Law, *The Antarctic Voyage of HMAS 'Wyatt Earp'*, Allen & Unwin, 1995, p. 11.

Natone on the rocks, 1959. Copyright unknown. Courtesy: Gympie Regional Library.

Life after the ice

Wongala   'the ship that won't give in'

Natone   'Just a little ship but she could tell an amazing story'

HMAS *Wyatt Earp* departed from Macquarie Island on 24 March 1948, returning to Port Melbourne on 1 April, 'the last sizeable ship of the RAN to use sail power'.[1] Although much of her ANARE voyage was deemed to be successful, it was clear that a larger ship was needed for future Antarctic expeditions. It was decided that HMAS *Wyatt Earp* would not be used for further Antarctic work and she was paid off on 30 June 1948.[2]

Leaving the RAN, *Wyatt Earp* became an asset and responsibility of the Department of Supply. Now almost 30 years old, both Commander Oom and Stuart Campbell spoke publicly about what a great ship *Wyatt Earp* was. But in reports, diaries and interviews they expressed the need for a 'roomier and more modern ship for exploration'.[3] Campbell believed that 'the day is past when any really useful work can be done by a vessel such as the *Wyatt Earp*, unless it be confined to surveying by small shore parties'.[4]

For three years *Wyatt Earp* lay alongside at Williamstown Dockyard, Melbourne. Then, in September 1951, reports that *Wyatt Earp* was for sale appeared. Under the heading, 'Historic ship up for sale', the *Melbourne Argus* reported:

93

> The most famous Australian exploration ship afloat, H.M.A.S. Wyatt Earp, is for sale.
>
> From yesterday anybody can tender for her with the Department of Supply.
>
> But shipping men doubt whether she is good for anything but Antarctic exploration.
>
> Her holds are too small to run her economically as a coastal ship, and her crew's quarters are unlikely to be approved by the Seamen's Union.
>
> Mr. P. G. Law, noted Australian Antarctic explorer said last night that to make her seaworthy the barnacles of three years would have to be scraped off and some seams above the waterline caulked.
>
> Her engines were perfect he said . . .
>
> Shipping men expect her to bring between £5,000 and £10,000.[5]

The Department of Supply advertised a tender for the purchase of 'H.M.A.S. *Wyatt Earp*—9th October, 1951. (Melbourne, Sydney, Adelaide, Brisbane, Perth and Hobart.)'[6] Further advertisements appeared in the *Commonwealth Gazette* and in newspapers around Australia, particularly in Tasmania.

Under the heading of 'Tenders' and the 'Department of Supply' the ship was described as 'Single Screw Motor Vessel H.M.A.S. *Wyatt Earp*. Located at Naval Dockyard, Williamstown, Vic.' Information given included that she was 'of heavy timber construction, metal sheathed to load waterline, the *Wyatt Earp* has a speed of 7 to 8 knots. Endurance, 7300 miles at 7 knots. Accommodation is available for 37 officers and crew.' The advertisements offered inspection by arrangement with the General Manager of the Dockyard, and that tenders would close on 9 October at 2 pm at the District Contract Board in Hobart. A brief description gave her tonnage, length, and breadth. The following listed equipment and engines were included:

Equipment:

two derricks: one 37ft. 6in., with working load of 2½ tons; one 26ft. 6in. 2-ton elec. windlass. 1-ton elec. winch. 2 Stockless anchors, 9 cwt.

each, and 210 fathoms 1in. chain cable. Oil fuel tanks, cap. 105 tons. Fresh water tanks, cap. 33½ tons.

Engines:

2-stroke Diesel main engine, Crossley Bros., type H.R.8,480 B.H.P., 325 R.P.M.

Diesel driven auxiliary engine, Crossley Bros., type B.W.B.I., combination elec. generating, air compressing and pumping; 14 B.H.P, 1000 R.P.M.[7]

With rather more journalistic licence than usual, the *Daily Commercial News and Shipping List* made up some historical information regarding *Wyatt Earp*'s wartime activities:

> Arrived here in mid-year [1939] as the international situation was at its most ominous. Antarctic voyages were forgotten as the world war began and the Japanese moved down through the islands.
>
> For four years the Wyatt Earp sailed tropical waters and performed just as creditably as she had done in the ice packs.
>
> She carried thousands of tons of Australian defence materials in a long period of uninterrupted war service.[8]

At this time in her life *Wyatt Earp*'s tropical experience in Australia was one eight-week voyage from Sydney to Darwin and return. She spent the remainder of the War in and around Adelaide, hardly tropical waters.

The successful tender came from the Arga Shipping Company of St Helens, Tasmania, for 'an undisclosed figure' according to the *Argus*[9] although £11,000 is suggested by Peter Worsley.[10]

The ship reappeared on 10 July 1952 under the heading 'Back to Sea as *Wongala*' (without any of the previous prefixes) in a report from the *Age* (Melbourne):

> There were fewer than a dozen people at South Wharf yesterday to watch the 400-ton auxiliary schooner Wongala raise her sails, slip into Port Phillip Bay and head for Bass Strait.

> Few people who saw her sailing down the Bay remembered that the Wongala, formerly known as the Wyatt Earp, was a veteran of five Antarctic expeditions.
>
> She was purchased from the Federal Government by an Australian syndicate last year and is going to Devonport, for a final overhaul before going on to the inter-State cargo run.[11]

And a few days later the *Advocate* in Devonport noted the renamed ship had arrived. Once again she was waiting, this time for survey (a compulsory inspection when a ship changes ownership to ensure seaworthiness and safety) before entering the Bass Strait trade[12]. More waiting, and on 29 July it was reported 'the intention was to place the auxiliary schooner *Wongala* on the slip at the week-end. However the tide was not high enough and slipping will be delayed until the spring tide on Friday week.'[13] All must have gone well because on 16 August *Wongala* was loading cement for Melbourne, and on 20 August:

> Trying hard to disguise her 33 years under a new coat of paint, 'the ship that won't give in' steamed into Melbourne yesterday.
>
> The 400-ton Wyatt Earp, veteran of six Antarctic expeditions, has a new name, and a new lease of life of 20 or 30 more years.
>
> Yet last year the old salts at Williamstown were saying: 'It's breaking-up yards for her'.
>
> The old salts said she was no good for a coastal trader—too slow and not enough cargo space.
>
> Then the Arga Shipping Company of Tasmania bought her, gave her extra sail for more knots, and a new cargo hold.[14]

Wyatt Earp had a new name, a new job and a new lease of life! By December 1952 her expected arrival in the Port of Bunbury, Western Australia, to load timber for Melbourne, was reported.[15]

In March 1953 *Wongala* was in Newcastle having arrived with a cargo of Tasmanian potatoes. She was expected to leave immediately for Melbourne with a general cargo. It was noted she 'is still rigged for sail and has 3321 square feet of canvas. … Her Chief Officer (Mr. L. Myer) said sails were rigged whenever there was a wind from four points on the bow. The sails gave a little extra speed and steadied the ship.'[16]

The following year, under the headline 'Polar Ship Now Supply Ketch', the *West Australian* informed readers that:

Wongala, Fremantle Wharf, 1952. Naval History Section—Sea Power Centre

> The former polar exploration vessel Wyatt Earp (400 tons), now named Wongala, is serving as a supply ketch, carrying explosives.
>
> The Wongala, an auxiliary ketch, is unloading thousands of cases of explosives at Woodman Point.
>
> The Wongala is one of the few wooden ships which use sail remaining on the Australian coast.
>
> In conjunction with her diesel engines, she uses sail during most of her voyages.[17]

For several years *Wongala* sailed the eastern and southern coasts of Australia, carrying a variety of cargo including potatoes to Sydney and iron and pressed wallboard from Newcastle to Tasmania. Its voyages can be tracked through the 'Shipping Lists' in newspapers that published such information on a daily basis. In 1954, the *Canberra Times* reported '*Wyatt Earp* Aground', while on a voyage to Port Moresby:

> The former Antarctic exploration ship, Wyatt Earp, went aground yesterday at Coconut Island, between Thursday Island and the Papuan coast.
>
> The ship, which is carrying a cargo of explosives and other equipment to be used by an oil search company in Papua, was aground for ten hours before being refloated on the high tide.[18]

Under the heading, 'Famous ship and old Rabaul-ite', the January 1954 issue of the *Pacific Islands Monthly* carried some of the history of the ship:

> Trading between Eastern Australia and New Guinea ports are a ship (the Wongala) and a first mate (Captain C. J. R. Webb, RAN) who both have an interesting history.
>
> The Wongala was formerly the American Antarctic exploration ship Wyatt Earp. She was built in 1919, and in the thirties she was acquired by the late Lincoln Ellsworth, famous explorer, for work in the Antarctic. Thenceforward, she was often in the news—especially in 1936, when Ellsworth and a companion crossed the Antarctic polar cap in a plane, and then disappeared. Two months later an Australian expedition found them holed up under deep snow at the

Bay of Whales, a few hours before the Wyatt Earp also arrived. Wyatt Earp became a Naval vessel during World War II.

Captain Webb was harbourmaster at Rabaul for 15 years, escaped from the Japs in 1942, and subsequently rendered distinguished service as a ship's commander under the Navy—especially in convoy and salvage work.[19]

The *Cairns Post* followed this with a lengthy heading: 'Adventurous Pair Visit Cairns—Sailor and Ship with a History—Echo of Polar Exploration' and the information that:

A ship and a sea-faring man that arrived in Cairns together at the week-end could provide enough material between them for several full length adventure novels.

The ship was the tiny Wongala, formerly known as the Wyatt Earp which, until about 14 years ago, was actively engaged in Antarctic exploration work.

The noted seafarer is Commander C. J. R. Webb R.A.N. 'S' (retired) who is chief mate aboard the Wongala for the duration of her present voyage from Sydney to New Guinea ports and return.

The Wongala—or Wyatt Earp—began to sail into the world's Press headlines when she was taken over by the famous American explorer Lincoln Ellsworth for adventuring in the Antarctic.

It was Ellsworth who bestowed the name of Wyatt Earp on her, to commemorate a sheriff of that name in his own home country.

Ellsworth commanded various expeditions to the Antarctic between 1933 and 1939 and on at least one of them, he was accompanied by the equally famous Sir Hubert Wilkins, Australia's polar explorer, who was organiser, meteorologist, photographer and reporter—all in one.[20]

The article concluded that although 'she was built in 1919 and might be described as ancient as a ship's age is reckoned, she is still splendidly sea-worthy and appears to be good for a long time to come.'

In 1956 the Sydney-Ulverstone Shipping Company bought *Wongala* for trading along the Queensland coast and for shipping cattle from Queensland to Papua-New Guinea. They changed her name to *Natone*, possibly after the potato-growing area around Ulverstone, on the northern coast of Tasmania.

The Australian Naval Intelligence Division located in Navy Office, Melbourne, in its 'Australia Station Intelligence Summary' (classified SECRET) in February 1957 noted:

> The interstate freighter 'WONGALA', formerly the Antarctic research ship 'WYATT EARP', has been sold to the Sydney-Ulverstone Shipping Pty Ltd., and renamed 'NATONE'.
>
> After a trip to Lord Howe Island, 'NATONE' has been engaged exclusively in the Sydney-Ulverstone trade.[21]

The *Pacific Islands Monthly* kept track of the ship, even after her last name change. At the end of 1957, finding work wherever she could get it, *Natone* was reported in Lautoka, Fiji, 'unloading flour from Australia'.[22]

In January 1958, not long after she returned from Fiji, *Natone* was carrying a cargo of vegetables from Hobart to Sydney. She made the newspapers again, referencing her back to *Wyatt Earp*, The headline shouted, 'Frantic Pumping Keeps Old Polar Ship Afloat'. *Natone* struggled into the port of Eden on the New South Wales south coast just before her main pump broke down. The *Canberra Times* reported:

> Engineers aboard the former Antarctic supply ship, *Wyatt Earp*, manned the ship's main pump in 3 ft. of water after the vessel sprang a leak in the Tasman Sea. ... While the ship was battling against heavy seas, numerous leaks occurred in the hold. The crew of 11 manned the ship's pump, but it was unable to jettison water as fast as the ship leaked. Three times the vessel almost foundered before it reached Eden. An almost superhuman effort by the crew, who worked in 3ft of water in the lower hold, kept the ship afloat.[23]

Natone berthed at Snug Cove, the Twofold Bay wharf at Eden. Two small auxiliary pumps were rushed from Sydney to save the ship. The report concluded that two surveyors from Sydney would decide if she could be made seaworthy. She must have been as there are no other reports of further disaster. The incident, however, served as an ominous warning of

Chapter 5　　　　　　　　　　　　　Life after the ice—*Wonga* and *Natone*

Natone, in Brisbane on 9 November 1957, loading salvage equipment to aid a vessel stranded on the Great Barrier Reef. Photograph taken by Colin Jones. Courtesy © David Jones.

the day (24 January), exactly twelve months later, when the ship would be grounded on a Queensland beach.

Repaired and cleared to sail again, *Natone* headed north. By early January 1959 she had delivered a shipment of cattle from Queensland to New Guinea and planned to return to Brisbane in ballast. *Natone* sailed from Lae, New Guinea, southbound. Under the heading, 'New Year Weather Havoc', the *Pacific Islands Monthly* reported: 'Fierce January weather brought floods to part of the Cooks Islands, the BSIP[24], and Fiji, and helped sink the freighter *Natone* north of Australia.'[25] The same edition of the journal noted, in a later paragraph, that *Natone* was 'on charter to a company in Papua—or had been (elsewhere)'.[26] Here, 'elsewhere' meant 'see elsewhere', and referred to *Natone's* so-called sinking (she actually ran aground) reported earlier in the magazine.

Sailing south along the Queensland coast *Natone* was hit by really nasty weather. She survived a week of storms The *Canberra Times* warned 'Two Cyclones Threaten Queensland', saying that:

> North Queensland was sandwiched between two cyclones about 1,500 miles apart tonight [Friday 16 January 1959].
>
> The Weather Bureau forecast for the next 24 hours is for flood-rains, high winds and rough seas.
>
> Warnings of storms ahead have been broadcast to ships lying along the entire coastline from Brisbane to Karumba, in the Gulf of Carpentaria.[27]

There are at least eight newspaper articles or websites with information regarding where *Natone* was travelling to, or from, at the time of her grounding. Four suggest south to north along the coast, another four give details of a north to south voyage. Considering the information available, it is certain *Natone* was travelling north to south, from New Guinea to Brisbane. This is supported by an article in *Bow2Stern* magazine, part of which reads:

> By 1959 she was in her fortieth year and the polar veteran was reduced to carrying cattle north to Papua-New Guinea. It was while returning in ballast from delivering such a cargo to Lae that the final chapter

of the old Wyatt Earp's story was written. January is the heart of the cyclone season and as the Natone forged her way south through the Coral Sea she met two of them.

For two weeks she struggled through monsoonal rain and cyclonic wind and seas. Her ancient seams opened off Cairns and she began to take water. By the time she reached Sandy Cape *Natone* was in dire distress. The water had risen 1.5 metres in her engine room, swamping her engines and cutting power. Sails were set, but she could barely make way and was driven inexorably towards the shore. The freighter Malekula attempted to help, but by then she was in shallow water.

At 10.15pm on Saturday night, 24 January 1959, *Natone* grounded near Mudlo Rocks at Rainbow Beach, 10 km north of Double Island Point. Throughout the night she was battered by the surf which smashed her only usable lifeboat. Her 18 Australian and New Guinea crewmen huddled on the focsle until growing daylight allowed them to surf onto the beach where all arrived safely. But the old *Natone* was finished. Beaten by the surf her timbers gave way and she soon broke up and disappeared beneath the waves.

Fanefjord; *Wyatt Earp*; *Wongala*; *Natone*: just a little ship, but she could tell an amazing story.[28]

The *Canberra Times* continued to take an interest in the story, under the headline, 'Violent Seas Wreck Former *Wyatt Earp*':

> Six European officers and 12 Papuans struggled 300 yds. through mountainous seas on wooden hatch-covers early to-day from their stricken ship *Natone* which foundered 120 miles north of Brisbane last night.
>
> They were swept half a mile along the beach before being hurled among jagged rocks.
>
> They reached safety after spending last night huddled in the forecastle while huge waves steadily ripped the wooden freighter to pieces.
>
> The *Natone*, formerly the Antarctic exploration ship *Wyatt Earp*, was bound for New Guinea [sic] from Brisbane.

> The grounding last night climaxed two weeks of battering from monsoonal rains and the tail ends of two cyclones.
>
> Her seams gradually opened yesterday afternoon.
>
> The engine room shipped 3 ft. of water, stopping the engines and pumps.
>
> Wallowing helplessly in huge seas her master, Captain P. H. Gooschalk, of Geelong, rigged emergency sails and *Natone* gradually crept towards the safety of a sheltered bay.
>
> However, unable to steer properly, *Natone* gradually drifted away from the bay and finally grounded near Mudlow [sic] Rocks, six miles north of Double Island Point.
>
> ...
>
> As the *Natone* grounded she listed 30 degrees to starboard and the waves immediately smashed one life-boat.
>
> The other could not be lowered because of the ship's list.[29]

The next day the *Canberra Times* followed up their story with 'Watchman on Wrecked Ship':

> A watchman to-day took up duty at the wrecked coastal ship *Natone* after crowds of sightseers flocked to Double Island Point for souvenirs.
>
> All day, a heavy surf tossed ashore wreckage and equipment off the ship, 300 yards from the beach.
>
> The seas were still too rough to permit an attempt at salvaging some of the ship's papers and documents.
>
> The Commonwealth Navigation Department deputy director in Brisbane, Captain W. Nicholson, said to-night a departmental inquiry into the grounding of the *Natone* would be held this week.[30]

Records of the inquiry have not been located. Many files have been destroyed as departments, likely to have been involved, have moved offices during the last sixty years.

Having been grounded and then completely wrecked by the surf, *Natone* remained where she was. Initially, depending on the tide, what was left of her could be seen. Many of her relics were salvaged, including the original ship's bell. This is now on display at the South Australian Museum and is engraved *Fanefjord* 1919 on one side and HMAS *Wyatt Earp* 1947 on the other.

The Inskip Peninsula Recreation Area, just south of Fraser Island, on the Queensland coast is home to the MV Natone camping area, named for the ship that was wrecked nearby. The website suggests 'You'll never want to leave this shady and secluded camping area that has front row seats to the beach and Great Sandy Marine Park. Set up camp under coastal sheoaks and Moreton Bay ash and take in the views towards Wide Bay Bar and Fraser Island.' Sounds a pleasant resting place for a special ship!

In 2009, the *Gympie Times* described the *Natone* as 'one of Australia's most famous ships', and reported on the re-emergence of the ship not seen for some years: 'Wild seas ripped into the Cooloola Coast last weekend eroding metres of sand from Rainbow Beach's fragile sand dunes but the erosion may have a positive side—unearthing what is thought to be one of Australia's most famous ships'. The article continued:

> The section of old ship wreck surfaced only 50 metres from the surf lifesaving tower on Rainbow's main beach.
>
> The large timber object is thought to be part of the hull of the Natone.
>
> The 450-ton Natone started out as the Wongala and was later changed to the Wyatt Earp and it was under this name this ship carried South Australian explorers Sir Douglas Mawson [sic] and Sir Hubert Wilkins on their famous voyages to the Antarctic.
>
> Voyages that put the Wyatt Earp and the explorers on the front pages of newspapers all over the world.[31]

Cautionary Tale

Found on several websites is a photo of a three masted vessel referred to as *Wyatt Earp* with the information that she was bought from the Australian government, and renamed *Wongala* by W. E. Tucker (later Tucker Shipping Co.). There certainly was a ship named *Wongala*, owned by W. E. Tucker, but she was not built in Norway in 1919! This three masted steel schooner was built in 1957 in the Cheoy Lee Shipyard in Kowloon, Hong Kong. She was slightly larger than *Wyatt Earp*, being 452 tons and 144 feet. And she was built to transport explosives around Australia and New Zealand, according to the South Australian Maritime Museum website. At the time she was built (1957) the *Wyatt Earp/Wongala* had already been renamed *Natone*, so presumably there was no problem with naming the new ship *Wongala*. The 'new' *Wongala* was wrecked on 22 July 1981, on Bett Reef in the Torres Strait.

Wongala but NOT the former *Wyatt Earp* at sea under full sail. Courtesy: Naval History Section—Sea Power Centre.

Chapter 5   Life after the ice—*Wonga* and *Natone*

Endnotes

1. John Bastock, *Australian Ships of War*, Angus & Robertson, 1975, p. 296.
2. www.navy.gov.au/sites/default/files/documents/Commonwealth_Naval_Orders_1948.pdf, p. 154.
3. *Age* (Melbourne), 2 April 1948, p. 3.
4. Group Captain Stuart Campbell's handwritten diaries held in the National Archives of Australia under NAA:P1557, 4 Item 840298.
5. *Argus* (Melbourne), 12 September 1951, p. 28.
6. *Commonwealth of Australia Gazette*, 20 September 1951, p. 2447.
7. As an example: *Examiner* (Launceston, Tas.) 22 September 1951, p. 20.
8. *Daily Commercial News and Shipping List*, 26 September 1951, p. 1.
9. *Argus* (Melbourne), 7 November 1951, p. 15.
10. Peter Worsley, 'HMAS *Wyatt Earp*' in *Maritime Heritage Association Journal*, Vol. 23 No.1 March 2012.
11. *Age* (Melbourne), 10 July 1952, p. 3.
12. *Advocate* (Burnie, Tas.), 15 July 1952, p. 2.
13. *Advocate* (Burnie, Tas.), 29 July 1952. p. 8.
14. *Argus* (Melbourne, Vic.) 20 August 1952, p. 3.
15. *South Western Times*, Bunbury,WA, 4 December 1952, p. 21.
16. *Newcastle Morning Herald and Miners' Advocate*, 3 March 1953, p. 2.
17. *West Australian*, 6 June 1953, p. 6.
18. *Canberra Times*, 7 January 1954, p. 4.
19. *Pacific Islands Monthly*, Volume XXIV No.6, Jan 1, 1954, p. 5.
20. *Cairns Post*, 4 January 1954, p. 4.
21. 'Australia Station Intelligence Summary' at www.navy.gov.au/sites/default/files/documents/ASIS_50_Feb_57.pdf
22. *Pacific Islands Monthly*, Vol. XXVIII No.5 (Dec 1,1957) p. 89.
23. *Canberra Times*, 24 January 1958, p. 1.
24. British Solomon Islands Protectorate
25. *Pacific Islands Monthly*, Vol. XXIX No.7, Feb 1,1959, p. 13.
26. *Pacific Islands Monthly*, Vol. XXIX No.7, Feb 1,1959, p. 101.
27. *Canberra Times*, 17 January 1959, p. 1.
28. David Jones from personal correspondence: the original of an article published in *Bow2Stern*, No. 16, December 2011.
29. *Canberra Times*, 26 January 1959, p. 1.
30. *Canberra Times*, 27 January 1959, p. 15.
31. www.gympietimes.com.au/news/wild-weather-unearths-aussie-ship/237734/.

Note: Image in chapter heading on page 93 shows Natone grounded near Mudlo Rocks. https://www.navy.gov.au/hmas-wyatt-earp

Grounded! *Natone* on the rocks, January 1959. Copyright unknown. Image courtesy Gympie Regional Library.

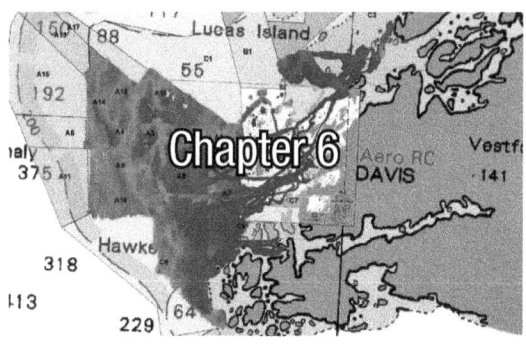

ASV (Antarctic Survey Vessel) Wyatt Earp

The Royal Australian Navy (RAN) and the Hydrographic Service Royal Australian Navy have had an involvement in expeditions to the Antarctic and sub Antarctic islands from 1911 when Morton Moyes (later Captain, RAN) joined Mawson's Australasian Antarctic Expedition (AAE) in 1911–14 as Mr Moyes. He was the meteorologist for the Western Base party under Frank Wild, and wintered on the Shackleton Ice Shelf. Moyes joined the RAN in 1914 as an instructor. In 1916 he was the navigating officer of *Aurora* under the command of Captain J. K. Davis, which sailed to rescue marooned members of Sir Ernest Shackleton's Trans-Antarctic Expedition. With his experience, it is not surprising that, in 1929, at Mawson's request, he was appointed as survey officer of Mawson's 1929–30 British Australian and New Zealand Antarctic Research Expedition (BANZARE) in Scott's ship, *Discovery*.[1]

A long and enduring link between the RAN and the Hydrographic Service with the Antarctic and the Australian Antarctic Division (AAD) was born and further cemented with the appointment of Lieutenant Karl Oom RAN as hydrographic surveyor/cartographer in *Discovery* for Mawson's 1930–31 BANZARE voyage. Oom, by then Commander, was Captain of *Wyatt Earp* on the first Australian National Antarctic Research Expedition in 1948–49.

In the early 1990s, somewhere in the many corridors of Navy Office bureaucracy, it was remembered there was a name without a ship, a name with a huge thick file, a name to be proud of, a name of service and of hard work and of Antarctic waters: the name—Wyatt Earp.

WYATT EARP: The little ship with many names

ASV *Wyatt Earp* cruising past Shirley Island, near Casey Station. © Martin Riddle. Courtesy: Australian Antarctic Division.

The RAN team of Glen Cooksey, Michael (Mick) Kumpis, Shaun McKee and Peter-John (Pete) Pedersen on the ASV *Wyatt Earp*. © Glen Cooksey. Courtesy: Australian Antarctic Division.

And, in 1993, Antarctic Survey Vessel (ASV) *Wyatt Earp* joined the Australian Hydrographic Service (AHS). Built by Pro Marine at Seaford, a suburb of Melbourne, on Port Phillip Bay, she is a survey launch, a smaller version of the Royal Australian Navy's Fantome class and built specifically for hydrographic survey work in the Antarctic. She replaced Survey Motor Boat (SMB) *Deliverance* which, after a surveying career stretching from 1974 to 1981, spent a further four seasons in the Antarctic with the Australian Hydrographic Service and the Hydrographic Office Detached Survey Unit (HODSU). The outcome of *Deliverance's* first Antarctic deployment in 1987 was the publication of the first metric chart AUS 600 of the Approaches to Mawson Station and Horseshoe Harbour.

Technical details for ASV *Wyatt Earp* include that she:

> has a full load displacement of 5.77 tonnes (5.68 long tons; 6.36 short tons), is 8.15 metres (26 ft 9 in) long at the waterline and 9.2 metres (30 ft 2 in) in length overall, and has a draught of 0.53 metres (1 ft 9 in). Propulsion is provided by two Volvo Penta AQAD 41D/SP290 diesels, which provide 400 brake horsepower (300 kW) to the two outdrives. Maximum speed is 22.5 knots (41.7 km/h; 25.9 mph), and *Wyatt Earp* has a range of 306 nautical miles (567 km; 352 mi) at 18 knots (33 km/h; 21 mph). When built, the boat's sensor suite includes a JRC JMA-2141 navigation radar, an STN Atlas Elektronik Deso 22 echo sounder, and a differential GPS receiver. *Wyatt Earp* has a complement of four to five.[2]

ASV *Wyatt Earp* can be transported on a trailer, and is usually stored at HMAS *Waterhen* in Sydney when not in use. She requires a resupply ship of the Australian Antarctic Division to transport her to the Antarctic and to serve as a base ship for her and her crew. From Kevin Slade's paper, 'Sounding South', we know that:

> In the period 1986 to 2003 surveys were conducted in the anchorages and approaches to Mawson, Casey and Davis Stations, at Buckles Bay and Hasselborough Bay at Macquarie Island and at Atlas Cove at Heard Island. These surveys along with passage sounding data

collected have been the basis for new metric large and medium scale charts for these locations.

More recently, ASV *Wyatt Earp* was deployed, in 2014, to Casey Station to conduct surveys of the offshore approaches to the base and, in 2017, to Davis Station, with new charts of both areas being produced. Renamed in 2010, the Deployable Geospatial Support Team (DGST) of the RAN Australian Hydrographic Service also deployed in 2018 and 2019 to conduct tidal work and approach surveys to the landings at Australia's three mainland stations.

The following article from the Australian Antarctic Division's on-line news 'This week at Davis: 24 February 2017'[3] gives an excellent picture of the work done by ASV *Wyatt Earp.*

Hydrographical surveys at Davis

The end of the boating season is fast approaching at Davis in what has been a successful season which began on the 9th of January 2017 for both Geoscience Australia (GA) (in the Division's workboat *Howard Burton*) and the Royal Australian Navy (RAN) (in the Antarctic survey vessel (ASV) *Wyatt Earp*). A total of 34 days of sounding has been accomplished so far, which encompasses the mapping of large areas offshore and to the north and south (112 km^2) which address both charting and scientific objectives, collection of 20 seabed samples, camera drops and 33 line km of sub-bottom profiles.

For those not familiar with Project 5093, it is a collaboration between the RAN, GA and the Australian Antarctic Division with the information we collect being used for safety of navigation in Antarctic waters and to support a range of scientific, environmental management and operational activities. In gathering this information we use a variety of equipment, including multi–beam echo sounders, sediment grabs, sub-bottom profilers and underwater cameras.

A typical day for the team begins at 0730 with the boats being lowered into the water by crane—an operation which took a bit of patience and ingenuity by personnel from both boats and the Division's plant operators.

The boats then transit to their particular survey area for the day's soundings or sampling, which may include one or more of the aforementioned equipment with the aim to be back alongside Davis wharf by 1700 for recovery and processing of the data.

What do we mean when we say sounding an area? The multi-beam echo sounder is our primary sensor used to measure depth, collect backscatter and water column data. We do this by driving the boat in 'lines', (also called mowing the lawn) to ensure that we achieve 100% coverage of a particular area. Once the area is completed we move onto the next. Some areas are larger than others and while some lines may only be a minute or two long, some are much longer and depending on wind, sea ice and sea state can be tricky to drive.

No matter the weather conditions for the day—overcast or clear—the scenery supplied by Antarctica out on the water is spectacular. Icebergs from small to very large in all different shapes and sizes with the most amazing colours provide much viewing pleasure and plenty of photo opportunities for team members and a few lucky personnel who have had the opportunity to come and spend a day out assisting us on the water.

There have also been times when those magnificent bergs are just sitting in the wrong spot—right where we need to drive the boat. Some of those bergs have moved along and we have been able to revisit areas and fill in the gaps left. Others will have to wait until the next hydrographic surveying teams visit Davis.

Although spectacular, there have been instances where the dangers of working in Antarctica have been reminded to us. We have witnessed icebergs roll over and break apart. There have also been times where we have had to return to station at the rush due to deteriorating weather conditions and sea ice floes threatening to make the wharf inaccessible.

There has also been plenty of wildlife to keep us entertained. From the endless supply of penguins to killer whales and seals. ASV *Wyatt Earp* was lucky enough to have a whale surface right next to her and we did see a pod with numbers around 12 swim by us while eating lunch, which along with the backdrop was extraordinary and something most people only get to see on a David Attenborough special.

Both vessels have had curious penguins join them on the back deck, just to make sure we were alert and doing our job properly. Luckily they decided against joining us in the cabin. We have all seen the elephant seals which like to block the road to the wharf, or play alongside it in the water with the occasional Weddell.

Boy, have there been plenty of ups and downs in the boats (puns intended), but the experience is one that not one of us will forget in a hurry. It is definitely a privilege to just come down here, but having the opportunity to work out on the water in this environment makes us some of the luckiest people.

Cooksey (Watercraft Operator)

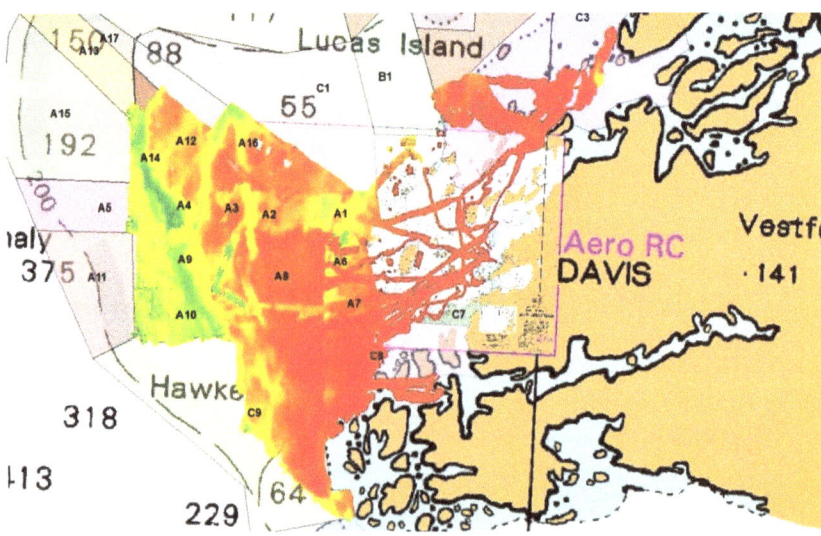

Results of the hydrographic surveying done in Prydz Bay.

Kevin Slade's paper concludes:

> Significant parts of the Australian Antarctic Territory and Sub Antarctic Islands in Australia's Charting Area (ACA) remain unsurveyed and with the increased numbers of tourist vessels visiting these southern waters there will be a need for hydrographic surveys to be undertaken to modern standards and charting coverage produced to ensure the safety of navigation of these vessels. The outcomes of such work also support scientific work undertaken during Australian Antarctic Division programs in further understanding the maritime environment of Antarctica.
>
> The Australian Hydrographic Service [and ASV *Wyatt Earp*] will continue to be part of this process.[4]

And so the chapters close on *Wyatt Earp, the little ship with many names.* Those who built her in 1919 could not possibly have foreseen where this ship would go or what she would achieve. Even Lincoln Ellsworth and Hubert Wilkins would have had little idea of the important role this ship would play in Australia's Antarctic ambitions in the years after they had taken her on four extraordinary voyages to Antarctica—the earth's coldest, windiest and iciest continent, with the surrounding seas also the coldest, windiest and iciest!

Endnotes

1. Lieutenant Kevin Slade RAN Ret, 'Sounding South—Hydrographic Surveying and Charting in Antarctica'. Information from this paper is quoted in this chapter with permission and support of 'Shotgun' Slade who died suddenly in January 2020, before this book was finished.
2. https://en.wikipedia.org/wiki/ASV_Wyatt_Earp
3. www.antarctica.gov.au/living-and-working/stations/davis/this-week-at-davis/2017/this-week-at-davis-24-february-2017. Courtesy Australian Antarctic Division.
4. Lieutenant Kevin Slade RAN Ret, 'Sounding South—Hydrographic Surveying and Charting in Antarctica', p. 8.

… and remembering the theme song for the television series starring Ellsworth's hero Marshal Wyatt Earp, this little ship was

**BRAVE, COURAGEOUS AND BOLD!
LONG MAY HER STORY BE TOLD!**

Bibliography

Andrews, Malcolm, *Hubert Who? War hero. Polar explorer. Spy. The incredible life of unsung adventurer Hubert Wilkins.* ABC Books, HarperCollins, 2011.

Bastock, John, *Australian Ships of War*, Angus & Robertson, 1975.

Bertrand, Kenneth J., *Americans in Antarctica 1775–1948*, American Geographical Society Special Publication No.39, 1971.

Burgess, Trish (ed.), *Bearing the Heart of a Sailor, Letters from the Antarctic and Other Faraway Places*, 2004.

Burke, David, *Moments of Terror. The Story of Antarctic Aviation.* Robert Hale, 1994.

Ellsworth, Lincoln, *Beyond Horizons*, Doubleday, Doran & Company, Inc., 1938.

Ellsworth, Lincoln, *Exploring Today*, Dodd, Mead & Company, 1935.

Law, Phillip, *The Antarctic Voyage of HMAS Wyatt Earp*, Allen & Unwin, 1995.

Lowell, Thomas, *Sir Hubert Wilkins: His World of Adventure, An autobiography recounted by Lowell Thomas,* Readers Book Club, 1961.

Maynard, Jeff, *Antarctica's Lost Aviator: The Epic Adventure to Explore the Last Frontier on Earth*, Pegasus Books, 2019.

Nasht, Simon, *The Last Explorer: Hubert Wilkins, Australia's Unknown Hero*, Hodder Australia, 2005.

Ommanney, F.D., *South Latitude*, Longmans, Green and Co., 1938.

www.ingramcontent.com/pod-product-compliance
Lightning Source LLC
Chambersburg PA
CBHW050929240426
43671CB00020B/2972